Funeral Foolishness

... a cry for help!

by Dr. I. Franklin Perkins

dpRochelle
PO Box 9523
Hampton, Virginia 23670
1 (757) 825-0030
ItsmeDrIFP.org

© 2017 Dr. I. Franklin Perkins. All Rights Reserved

No part of this book may be reproduced, stored in a retrieval system, or transmitted by any means without the written permission of the author.

First published by dpRochelle 4/29/17

ISBN: 978-0-9862389-4-9

Printed in the United States of America, Hampton, Virginia

Dedication

Dedicated to those who thought about it but couldn't say it.
I promise you . . . I will!

Epigraph

"I used to think that it was people of whom I grew tired but later discovered that it was actually their choice of being unenlightened that vexed me the most."

Dr. I. Franklin Perkins

Acknowledgments

Always thanks to my husband, Pastor Derrick, Sr., my son, Derrick, Jr. and my daughter, Aegious for allowing me to be me

Thank you Book Reviewers!

Thanks to my editors:

Dr. Arnita Snead Brooks
Rev. Luther S. Allen, III

Preface

Well, this has been a long time coming, but here we are. I will say on the outset, that I am especially proud of this work and feel quite at ease as I flow across the keyboard of my computer.

Some "religious folks" will feel that this book is an outrage and should not have been written, yet, it will bring awareness to some of the ills that plague the African American culture through the eyes of my personal experiences and shared information from others. On the other hand, some may find this material hilariously comedic and will perhaps desire to see it aired on television for their future amusement. Whichever way it is perceived, it is necessary to understand that this book has been developed partly to expose foolishness but mostly for educational enhancement.

In either circumstance, these stories are depictions of ridiculous aggravations and some embellished anecdotal situations associated with them. Hopefully, the reader will glean the lessons to be learned as a result.

Introduction

Welcome to a collection of accounts of unscrupulous behaviors experienced during the passing of loved ones. After many years of eulogizing, attending and officiating funeral services of friends, family and foes it has been discovered that a variety of situations which occurred before, during and after the services had little to do with respecting the deceased or their wishes. It is unfortunate that anyone would be subject to this type of imprudence yet the contents aforementioned dictate otherwise.

What exactly is the protocol for communicating with someone who has just lost a loved one? What is the role of each person involved? Who has the first say, the final say, any say in the planning of the conclusive resting place of the deceased? How does one account for in-laws, outlaws and by-laws during this crucial time? What is the correct way to memorialize that special someone? These questions and more will be addressed throughout the contents of this book.

Although this is written as a source of morbid laughable entertainment, understand that this type of satirical drama exists. Like something straight out of a scene of "Kingdom Come" or "Death at a Funeral" these events will have you in awe of the horrific attitudes displayed during periods of grief but will hopefully prevent you from responding in like manner.

It is to this end, that the array of professionals in the vocation of funeral services (whom shall remain nameless) were interviewed in order to acquire a conglomeration of these exaggerated events. Therefore, the book discusses situations from various perspectives designed to bring awareness to unhealthy behaviors. The latter information is to educate and assist those who desire and need order in a time of chaotic uncertainty, including helpful tips concerning the grieving process, insurance, wills, durable power of attorney, advanced medical directive, funeral protocol including sample obituaries and programs to empower and prepare the reader for the inevitable.

Further, it is a call for the melodramatic folks - those who wreak havoc by superimposing their will on others during this time of reflection, to stop the Funeral Foolishness-!

Funeral Foolishness

... a cry for help!

Table of Content

1   Chapter 1
       From My Perspective

15   Chapter 2
       From the Funeral Director's, Family, Friend's and Clergy's Perspective

33   Chapter 3
       Life Insurance

45   Chapter 4
       Samples of Final Arrangement Documents

121   Chapter 5
       Sample of Obituaries and Service Bulletins & Poems

Chapter 1
From My Perspective

Losing a loved one is never easy. If you loved them, it will break your heart to see them go, knowing that you will never physically see or touch them again. On the other hand, if for some reason you are glad that they are gone, O well, then that is something else that you will also have to work through. There is an empty space that is left once someone passes that no one else can fill; that moment, between the time you find out that they are gone until the time that they are buried, one will encounter an amalgamation of emotions, some positive and some negative. Let's take a look at the grieving process.

The Grieving Process

It is known that each person may grieve differently and their responses to losing a loved one may not mirror particular reactions experienced by others. In her book, *After the Storm Workbook/Journal (Recovering from Personal Loss and Grief)*, T. B. Williams discusses the five areas of grief. There are some online materials that debate that there are seven areas of grief but for the purposes of this writing we will only examine five areas.[1] It is necessary to know that people may go in and out of these various areas of grief with no particular order.

One area is <u>Denial</u>. This area of grief can possibly start during the time a person is grieving a loved one who is suffering from a terminal illness or perhaps awaiting the foreseeable demise. Although this may seem premature, knowing that the loved one is living out their last days could cause the reaction of disbelief and denial. Many began a meltdown during this step as they feel that they do not know what they would do without the individual in their life anymore. So they began to make up scenarios such as: they may continue to talk about the person as if they are coming home that night and also make future plans including the individual. They will soon discover that memories will be the only thing that they will have left to cherish.

Another area is *Anger*. After one has come to grips that the loved one is indeed gone, and not simply on a long vacation, anger sets in. There have been many shapes of anger from cursing others, throwing things to killing someone else to try and ease the pain. There was a woman

---

[1] T.B. Williams. *After the Storm Workbook/Journal (Recovering From Personal Loss and Grief)*, 1st Edition, Copyright 2012.

who was angry with everyone with whom she felt was responsible for the loss of her father. He fell ill, was put on life support and died. Of course, there was no one responsible for his death, as he was well over seventy years old and not in the best of health. However, the woman directed her anger at friends who did not call or visit, family members who seemed to be doing well in spite of the recent loss and anyone who she felt could have kept her father alive. This process could take some time to move through, as each person is different.

There is also the area of _Bargaining_. This is the time that some will begin to rationalize what could have been done to turn the outcome around . . . *"If I came home sooner I could have found him in time;" "if I had only call her last night . . . ;" "if I had taken her out of town with me . . ."* are just a few thoughts that may cross the minds of those going through this step. It was at this point in the grief process that a man bargained with God to keep his mother alive in exchange for his undying service that he would give God for the rest of his life. His loved one died anyway then he fell into a deep depression because he felt God let Him down.

The fourth area is _Depression_. This is where the woman mentioned in the second area of *Anger* got stuck.

Her depression had even led to thoughts of suicide because she felt alone and that no one loved her but her father, and now he was gone. She was not in the best of health either but refused to accept the fact that her father died. She was sad some days and then back to angry on other days which led to her becoming heavily medicated. Others have felt some degree of regret if they did not honor a request from the deceased which also led to depression.

The fifth area is _Acceptance_. When a person gets to this point it does not mean that they have it all together. It simply shows acknowledgement that something major has taken place and things will not be the same since the loved one is no longer present. This is a time to pick up the pieces and move forward. Things may not be 100% alright, but it is a place where a person can crossover into a place where they can function at a level that is acceptable. A reorganization of life's necessities will assist in a smoother transition, for one must supplement for the void that has been made. There was a man that lost his wife after several years of marriage who handled these areas in such a remarkable way that it was difficult to tell if he was grieving. After the funeral I asked about his well-being since he was now alone. He responded how he had taken care of his wife for many years through health and in sickness and that he had grieved throughout her illness and when she died he had no regrets because he had done everything that he knew to do for her. He was one of the first if not the only person that I have witnessed with this type of grief.[2] I realized that some people spread their jam around on the bread and others just plop it down in one glob; he obviously was a spreader.

These areas are not exhaustive and can be experienced over and over again without going through a complete cycle. I say again, each person reacts differently to loss and cannot adhere to a specific timeframe to move through it. It is not expected, however, that during this process a person should unnecessarily act out foolishly or break the law as a result.

It's My Prerogative

There are many things that will need to be considered after the loss of a loved one. What does a spouse do after losing the love of their life? For many years I have heard some unsettling comments concerning this area, one of which is the time frame in which a spouse remarries. Well, that is completely up to the individual

---

[2] Ibid.

who is getting remarried. No one can tell an individual what is too soon or too late to remarry. If they choose another mate after six months or after ten years, it is completely to the discretion of that person. There is no written rule that dictates a length of time however a person should ensure that they have actually completed at least 90% of their grief cycle before remarriage. Persons who remarry sooner than they are emotionally ready could result in one seeking a replacement instead of a mate. This action would place unnecessary expectations and demands on the new spouse that they cannot fulfilled.

If remarriage is after six months of the loss, it doesn't mean that they did not love their spouse nor does it mean that they were dating the other person while their spouse was living. Perhaps they could just be lonely? Maybe they enjoyed married life so much that they no longer desire to be single again? This is not anyone's call nor should anything be suspiciously directed at the individual who may still be grieving.

There were three brothers and one sister who lost their mother to illness. Their father married another woman within six months of burying his wife which infuriated at least two of the children. They were angry and felt as though their father should not have remarried, not just because it was a few months, but not at all. Each of his grown children was married with their own children. All of them could go home to someone but they expected their father to stay alone and single. How selfish was this? This is utter foolishness. It was their father's choice! No one was qualified to explain how he felt going home to an empty house. Consequently, he remarried someone with whom he felt was good for him. It is not about how anyone else feels it is what the individual who is involved desires.

Remarriage and the Spouse

Another negative comment made about the remarriage of a spouse is, who they decide to marry. Many people try to play matchmaker when not qualified to make these selections, especially if their relationship is not the best. One may think that they know who should be married to who but that would require expert knowledge in the lives of each individual which no one has. Is it possible to just let people live their lives to select the person with whom they are most comfortable? One cannot pick someone for another person simply on appearance or to meet their expectations; no one else will have to live with the final decision. If the spouse is happy with whom they have selected, then let the church say, "Amen!"

One lady was married to a pastor for a few years and was sorely mistreated. A few months after her husband passed away, many people wanted her to find another pastor to marry. She said, *"if a man asks her out and he tells her that he is a pastor, she would scream to the top of her voice and run in the other direction!"* With that being said, no one can possibly select someone for another; that choice is theirs and theirs alone.

Opinionated Banter

One of the selfish statements that I've heard relating to the death of an individual is, *"they died too soon."* What really is dying too soon? Perhaps a child of five, ten or twenty years old, may be a strong defense, but if a person is ninety-five years old, what is really too soon? They have lived a full life. It is understood that we do not want any of our loved ones to die but we all will eventually have to go sometime, no one is exempt. So, when is the best time to die? Can that question honestly be answered? This is not to be insensitive but truthful. Keep in mind that the person may have wanted to die when they did.

Who's In the Coffin?

Another issue that could use some maintenance is the misrepresentation of the life lived by the deceased; I gather this behavior is practiced in hopes of comforting the family. I have attended numerous funerals that the eulogizing person would speak kindly over the remains, in some cases even if they did not know the deceased. They recite flowery words of grace and sweetness as if the individual literally walked on water their whole life, when actually they were a slacker and a ball of combustible brimstones with everyone who knew them, obviously barring the one who was eulogizing the deceased.

In a case like this, the children were confused by the nice accolades attached to the name of their deceased father. As the pastor was speaking so well over the deceased, one of the sisters leaned over and said to her brother, *"Who in hell is in that coffin! It can't be our daddy because the pastor said he was a great father and nice to everybody – and we know that is not true."* It would be fabulous to talk to a few family members to learn something about the individual if one is the eulogizer. A list to follow would be to: find a close family or childhood friend who would candidly share stories of the deceased; a neighbor; a co-worker; people from any organization in which the deceased may have participated and/or a church member. This prior research can keep the eulogy true and relevant while avoiding embarrassment.

Where Are They?

Another misconception stems from the question, *"where does my loved one go when they die?"* Well, I believe that there is a heaven and a hell, and those who accept Jesus go to heaven and those who do not, well; they become a resident of the other place. On the basis of the former, it should be noted that everyone who dies is not a candidate for heaven no matter how we feel about them. It is rather amazing that we so often determine the final destination of someone who dies based on our feelings about them. If we never had a challenge with them we automatically feel that since they were pretty cool they are on their way to heaven. If we were envious of them or did not care much for them, then, according to us, they are automatically burning in hell with the devil, as if we have a say in anybody's final destination; it is not up to us.

Often those who reflect and speak over the remains may say how they know that the deceased is in heaven looking down at us or they know that they are singing in the heavenly choir. Statements of this magnitude dictates that we have the last say over the deceased, which are just words spoken without heart knowledge. We cannot build the outcome on our feelings. Consequently, we can speak good words of what we have witnessed and of what we have knowledge, such as: how faithful they were to service; how involved they were with the community; they unselfishly gave of their finances, a song they loved to sing; how much love they showed for their family; how much they enjoyed cooking; how they didn't minced words but were very straight forward with people; how often they exercised or if they loved a specific type of food. We should be mindful of what we say about the deceased as it will be a memory that will not be so soon forgotten.

Social Service Cancellations

In many states a person who is receiving assistance from social service may be qualified for burial assistance. It is suggested that you contact your state agency to determine if this benefit is available locally. In researching this information, I have discovered that a few of the states have ceased to offer burial assistance because of budget cut backs but it will be worth checking your particular state.

If the loved one is a recipient of food stamps (EBT card) or other services from the state please ensure that the necessary departments are contacted to report the death of the individual to avoid someone from fraudulently using their benefits. There was a case like this to happen with a man, who was living separate from his disabled spouse. She was able to get food stamps and other assistance from the state. When she passed, her sons were in possession of some of her property and her EBT card and were gearing up to use it until it expired. They bragged to family members and friends that they were going to make good use of it. When the spouse got wind of his stepsons fraudulent intentions he immediately called social service to make them aware of the death of his spouse and cancelled all services that she was receiving.

As we are addressing the cancellation of active services that the deceased may have had, it is wise to cancel all credit cards, and return all checks that are received after the date of death, in order to keep these items out of the hands of those who would be tempted to commit fraud.

Memorial Service

Memorial services are on the rise as cremations are used as an alternative means of memorializing their loved ones. This is when there isn't any physical body present for the service, only pictures or even perhaps the bottled cremated remains are present. Although cremation may or may not be the alternative for burial because of cost, it is economical for those who have limited means of handling the unavoidable. It will be completely your choice.

These types of dedications can be quicker than the traditional funeral service. If you intend to memorialize a loved one in a provocative manner, ensure that the facility of use will allow such practices prior to your plans. If a church setting is desired, please be respectful to the institution in which is chosen.

You may ask, why was this book written? It was written to increase awareness and to decrease funeral foolishness.

Chapter 2
From the Funeral Director, Family, Friend and Clergy Perspective

From the Funeral Director's Perspective

This task was an interesting "undertaking." As I randomly selected the various funeral directors to interview throughout the country, I found that most of them had similar tales of situations that were laughable, sad and yes, foolish. When I began my interview I asked the director, if they had dementia or Alzheimer's, what funeral story would they always remember, in spite of their mental ailment? At that moment the interview took off!

Although the funeral business is lucrative, it does not come without the ills of life that could impact the bottom line. In a place where business is "always dead" dramatic events may often make one wonder should they have gone to school for something else. Some of the Funeral Directors that shared their experiences for this book admitted that they were born into the business through a family legacy and the gift of burying the dead was bestowed upon them. Some had a desire to genuinely comfort families during one of the most horrific events that anyone could ever face, which is burying a loved one. Even though there were amalgamations of reasons for entering this type of business, I soon discovered that unnecessary drama was not one of them.

Four Minus Two is Two

A funeral director who has since retired shared that he has often served as a referee, a punching bag and a mediator. One of his unforgettable experiences involved a family of four siblings who had just lost their mother. Unfortunately, mother left zero paperwork behind to assist her family with her final arrangements. Thinking that the four grown children could get along just long enough to agree on a few necessary items, it never happened. Two of the children wanted to cremate mother and the other two children wanted to bury mother. He said that they began to say some awful things to one another that should never have been said to either family or another human being. They argued and cursed each other so badly that the funeral director asked if they would go home and discuss it and come back when they had come to an agreement. One of the children told the funeral director that they will have a decision shortly because he was going to kill the two siblings that will not agree with him.

Who Knew?

One funeral director out west was eager to get some things off of his chest. He had been in business for over twenty-seven years and explained how it is not always the families that bring the drama; sometimes it's the funeral home. He continued to say, that he had a family that desired a memorial service with their loved ones body present and then desired the body to be cremated afterwards. Somehow that message was not conveyed to the entire staff as the body was cremated prior to the service. Understanding that mistakes can happen, they went on with their memorial plans despite the absent body.

Paying Family

According to one director she shared that having a family bully is a regular activity at her funeral home. She stated that there is always one person that gives all of the directions, has all of the ideas and thoughts of what should be done for the deceased. When asked who they are they boldly say, *"I'm family!"* The director's response was, *"I understand that you are family but are you paying family?"* Of course, that shut down that voice and the person who was paying began to speak.

I Got This

A similar situation happened with another director. A widow was on her way to the funeral home to plan her husband's final arrangements based on the preneed information that she had and her grown stepchildren, who never visited their father before he became ill, wanted to come along. As the widow spoke to the director about various items one of the stepchildren interrupted her conversation with the director and demanded to know just how much the final arrangements were going to cost. The widow interrupted and asked the stepdaughter was she going to contribute anything to the final bill? At that moment the stepdaughter realized that she had overstepped her boundaries, quickly backed off and sat quietly for the rest of the appointment. The director's advice to those reading is, to avoid letting family, friends and other folks who are not paying for anything have a primary say in the final arrangements of your loved one. When the bill comes due, they will not be anywhere around.

It would also help if the family had a discussion of responsibility before visiting the funeral home. Because everyone's emotions may be all over the place during this time, this is a good reason to have preneed arrangements in order. It will also avoid misunderstandings in who will be responsible for bill.

How Could You

While we are discussing the final bill, another director discussed poor decisions made on the behalf of the family. A woman lost her husband and he did not have any insurance. After the funeral services, the widow still carried a rather large bill but made payment arrangements to pay off the balance. Soon after the services, other family members that were at odds with the widow wanted to purchase a headstone for their deceased family member but never inquired of the widow the balance that was left on the overall account. If they had pulled together, the balance could have been paid, but they opted to pull in multiple directions and no one achieved their goal.

Poor decisions causes everyone involved to lose. Where is the family when you need them?

What Are You Trying to Prove?

A funeral director expresses how often she deals with people who insist on inserting themselves into every family that has a funeral. She explains, for whatever reason some people always try to take whatever attention they can get through the lives, or in this case, the death of others. The director tells the story of how she had to pull someone out of the family line up before the family walked into the church. The person jumped in the line between the children and grandchildren which upset some of the children. They began to use unhappy language toward the person and almost came to blows because they made up a relationship just to insert themselves into the family. It is ostentatious and disrespectful to those who may still be grieving.

From the Family's Perspective

During the time of loss the family suffers the most. It is unfortunate that internal sabotage is often experienced from family members. One unfortunate situation occurs when a deeply buried family secret is placed in a coffin with the deceased, in hopes that it will remain entombed. Sadly, this rarely happens. It is not unheard of to find out that daddy is not really daddy at all but really the uncle of his brothers children. Or discovering that your uncle is also your daddy has caused fights to take place because the truth was withheld from them.

In modern times, most do not count on the word of family members anymore as it has become a pastime to have DNA testing done through Ancestry.com by spitting in a tube or allow Labstogo to draw blood to determine paternity, maternity or family relationships. It is not fair to withhold this information from those who are involved. This is deep water for so many and deserves a book all to itself.

Made From the Same Stock

There is another situation that a family felt was rather disheartening but unfortunately happens more often than not. A man that was well-known in his town died at the age of sixty-nine years old. The day of the funeral after the service, people were walking up to the coffin to pay their last respects to the deceased. A woman with two small children walked up to the coffin crying and beating the coffin with her fist. She turned around and the widow, sitting on the front pew caught a glimpse of the woman and the two children. She noticed that both of the children looked unmistakably like her own children and bore a strong resemblance to her deceased husband. The crying woman smirked at the widow and walked off with her children. The widow walked up to the coffin and slapped the face of her deceased husband as she knew that the rumors were true that he had another family somewhere else. Those children were his.

Something to Remember You By

Sometimes families do not have all of the finances that they need to bury their loved. One may ask for donations from others, or even take up an offering during the funeral services to pay for funeral services.

There was a family who were scrambling to get money to bury their family member. No one spoke up about any finances that would be helpful. However there was a family member quietly sitting close enough to hear everything but far enough to avoid any financial obligation, watching everything but saying nothing. After the services were over, that family member asked for a copy of the death certificate just so they can have something with Aunt Rose's name on it and to have something to remember her by. Unbeknownst to the others, that family member had a $30,000 policy on Aunt Rose for years and just needed the death certificate to claim the money. Even though a death certificate can be purchased from outside sources after 30 days, it would be more convenient for the policyholder to obtain one through the family or funeral home.

Now before a conclusion is drawn, please know that the family member has every right to stay quiet about the policy. If they paid for it, it belongs to them to do as they choose. They cannot be held liable for funding the funeral if they are not the responsible party. It would be nice if something is offered but some would take that as a license to overspend on unnecessary services offered on the menu because someone else is responsible. Food for thought, if someone asks for a death certificate, chances are, they have a policy on the deceased.

Not My Responsibility

Another person had a brother who was a "dead beat everything." He wouldn't pay his bills, always wanted handouts from his family and continued to be evicted from anywhere that he stayed. He was an alcoholic and was not a responsible person. He died at the age of fifty-two years old. His older brother found out about his death a few days later but refused to go and claim his body. He felt that his brother never took responsibility for anything in his life even down to life insurance. He knew that if he had claimed the body that he would be responsible for paying for the final arrangements. This infuriated him because he felt that his deceased brother was at it again and would have the upper hand on him even in death. So, he never went to claim the body and the State buried him.

Sorry, I Can't Help You

Sometimes people have a variety of reasons why they do what they do during times of grief. It is always easiest to say what we would do when we are not the ones to make the decision. Like in the case of a seventy-five year old woman who went on a Caribbean cruise vacation for 30 days. As she was three days into her trip, she received a call from a family member to tell her that her eighty year old husband died from a heart attack. When she was asked of her date of return, she advised the family member to go ahead and bury him because she has twenty-seven days left on her cruise and she did not want to lose her money.

From the Friend's Perspective

Secret Squirrel

Friends are often called upon to organize funeral services in the absence of family and sometimes in the presence of family depending on their abilities to get things done. In this case, Jon, a single man, who died from a heart attack, had no family to bury him. One of his friends stepped up to assume the responsibility for the burial expenses. The friend worked closely with the funeral home to ensure that his friends' final arrangements were orderly.

Once the day of the funeral arrived there was a major disturbance in the chapel. There were quite a few women angrily discussing who was going to sit on the front row. Unknown to the friend, Jon had multiple girlfriends and managed to keep them all apart throughout the span of his life but they all showed up for the final service. As many as there were, neither of the women knew about each other.

After a few minutes of finger pointing, a fight broke out. The women turned the chapel into an event that would bankrupt a WWE match. Shoes, wigs and purses were flying everywhere. They tussled, spit, pulled hair, clothes, and scratched one another. One of the women landed inside the coffin with the body. It makes perfect since why Jon died of a heart attack.

Nobody Like Momma

It is said that we should cherish our mother because we only have just one. Even though there are quite a few things that we only have just one of, for the sake of this story I will agree with the above statement; we only get one mother, so cherish her.

There was a son who would not respect his mother. He mistreated her for many years and cursed at her whenever they talked. The mother died and the son had a nervous breakdown when he discovered that she was gone. The doctor had to prescribe the son medicine in order for him to get through the funeral process and services because he could not control his grief. He couldn't eat, sleep, he became ill and was feeling remorseful for his actions towards his mother. After the burial was over, he did not want to leave his mother there by herself. Every day he was found lying on his mothers' grave crying and apologizing for not treating her better. It never crossed his mind that his mother would not live forever. This could have ended differently he could have treated his mother much better than he had.

From the Clergy's Perspective

Often, the clergy are directly involved with the planning and execution of funeral services in conjunction with the funeral home to ensure a smooth transition. However, one cannot account for everything that could occur during this time of preparation. Who can know the mindset of each family member and how they will grieve their loss? Unfortunately, some clergy have found out the hard way and have been victims of family fights and disagreements.

Wardrobe Gone Bad?

One pastor of over twenty-two years of pastoring received news that the chairman of his deacons' ministry sister passed but the news did not come from the deacon. He waited and waited for the deacon to share information with him about the service but he could never reach the deacon. He thought that this was rather strange because he and the deacon were very close, so he thought. The pastor saw the obituary write up in the paper and let other members of the church know the arrangements so they could support the deacon. The service was held at the local funeral home and another preacher was asked to eulogize the deacons' sister.

The preacher began to read the scripture and from out of nowhere the children of the deceased jumped up and started fighting each other. One of them hollered, *"How could you bury momma in a sweat suit!"* After the service, the deacon walked up to his pastor and said, *"I didn't want to tell the church about the funeral service because I knew my family was crazy and would embarrass me!"*

Unexpected Ambush

Another pastor of over twenty years of pastoring was providing bereavement care to a church member who had just lost her husband. She did not have children of her own but she did have stepchildren who were not her biggest fans since she married their father. As the pastor and widow talked about the services, the doorbell rang and the stepchildren barged into the house and ambushed the pastor as they beat the widow unmercifully. They were led to believe that their father left them some money and that his wife was holding out on them. The pastor said, *I did not sign up for this."*

Graveside Activity

A pastor of over ten years of pastoring eulogized a young man around the age of twenty-five years old at the graveside. Once the pastor finished the eulogy, the family wanted to open the coffin to say their last goodbyes. The kids began to throw different items in the coffin with the deceased. While everyone was participating, a young lady, who was rather drunk said, *"I didn't bring anything to leave with you, but here, you can have these."* She pulled off her underwear and threw them in the coffin with the deceased. The pastor said, *"No matter what I do, I cannot unsee that!"*

Graveside Drama

There was a woman who was not on speaking terms with her mother and moved away without any contact for over thirteen years. She received a call that her mother had passed. The daughter reluctantly returned home only to maintain her bitter and evil demeanor for the entire time towards the rest of the family. It was only until the lowering of the coffin in the ground that she totally lost her cool and broke down. She laid across her mothers' coffin and asked, *"Why did you leave me, take me with you, momma, don't go, take me with you."* The funeral director grabbed the woman and told her to cool it and that the family wanted her to leave the cemetery. As she walked away, she looked back at the mother's coffin and said, *"It's been real nice talking with you, call me sometime."*

Free Money

There was a teenager who died from a gunshot wound. He had the back of his head blown off as he stood in a phone booth. Needless to say, the church was packed to its capacity with many people and community groups representing. The family asked for the casket to be opened at the exit for final farewells. A few guys walked up to the body and dropped multiple $100 dollar bills in the casket.

As the family started to leave the church for the cemetery, the mother of the deceased teenager told her limo driver to call ahead and stop the hearse and then let her out of the car. When she got out of the car, she told the mortician to open the casket. He asked her why, was something wrong? She stated, *"Did you see all those $100 dollar bills they put in the casket? Well, I sure could use it now to pay my bills. I promise you, he can't use it where he's going!"* She grabbed all the money and walked back to the limo to continue the funeral procession to the cemetery.

Cough It Up, Pastor

There are many churches who try to assist their members who may not be able to bury their loved ones because of the absences of insurance. Unfortunately, not all recipients are appreciative of what can be done. So it was in the case of this small church.

The matriarch of a family died without insurance therefore the church stepped in to assist the family since the woman was a long standing member. When the pastor sat with the family and asked about the funeral plans she was told that the family did not have any insurance and would like to have help getting the cheapest burial arrangements possible. The pastor coordinated with the funeral home and the members who agreed to help with the most basic burial plans; they were able to gather all of the money needed to bury the woman but something else happened. After the family was told that the church had the money for the burial, the son of the deceased decided that he wanted a more expensive coffin for mother, more limousines for family and friends, 100's of multi-paged full color bulletins, which would have been an additional $4000 that the church would have had to raise; all while the family contributed zero dollars for their mother. The son was heard saying, *"If they can come up with the first amount, they can surely come up with an extra $4,000!"* Of course, that didn't happen.

Would He Want to Be Here?

Generally churches are helpful to all people. It has been in recent years, that churches have had to update their policies and bylaws to avoid law suits and unscrupulous activities that often darken the doorsteps. Because of the forced upgrades by the government and other outside entities, many churches are becoming strict in their policies as it relates to members and non-members, which is a segue to the following. A large percentage of pastors expressed their experiences when a church member loses a family member who is not a member of the church. In some cases it has caused families to leave the church or stay and become very bitter with the leadership or angry with the church as a whole. *This is because they expect the benefits that they receive from the church to transfer over to their non-member family.* It has been more often than not that families insist on having a funeral in a church for someone who never wanted to go to church when they could attend. Many funeral homes are equipped for various types of services and have adequate space to house the guest. Also, they often have fewer rules than organizations or churches that have policies to dictate operations. This situation begs the question, if the deceased didn't come to church when they were alive, would they want to lay in the church when they are dead? Another question that deserves an answer is, if the deceased wore jeans and sneakers all the time when they were alive, why bury them in a suit and tie that was borrowed from someone? It is noticed that the family often imposes their will on the deceased, especially if there aren't any instructions left for guidance.

Chapter 3
Life Insurance

If you have had the opportunity to visit any cemetery, you would find that there are long and short graves present. Although we feel that children have their whole life ahead of them, it cannot be assumed that they will live to be twenty-one. Children and teenagers are dying too and in many settings at an alarming rate.

We see the rise of fundraising sites such as go fund me, which gives the social community an opportunity to share their philanthropy with the needy and has helped thousands of people to meet a plethora of medical expenses. Sometimes the money is spent for other stuff instead of the initial purpose. However, when a parent can afford to buy their 10 year old child $200 tennis shoes and all the name brand clothing but will not pay $10 per month for a $25,000 basic life insurance policy for their most prized possession, it is beyond my level of comprehension and a foolish mismanagement of money. We must ask ourselves, what is really important?

Life insurance is a protection against financial loss that would result from the premature death of an insured. The named beneficiary receives the proceeds and is thereby safeguarded from the financial impact of the death of the insured. The death benefit is paid by a life insurer in consideration for premium payments made by the insured. Life insurance is a contract between an individual with an insurable interest and a life insurance company to transfer the financial risk of a premature death to the insurer in exchange for a specified amount of premium.

The goal of life insurance is to provide a measure of financial security for your family after you die. So, before purchasing a life insurance policy, consider your financial situation and the standard of living you want to maintain for your dependents or survivors. For example, who will be responsible for your funeral costs and final medical bills? Would your family have to relocate? Will there be adequate funds for future or ongoing expenses such as daycare, mortgage payments and college? It is prudent to re-evaluate your life insurance policies annually or when you experience a major life event like marriage, divorce, the birth or adoption of a child, or purchase of a major item such as a house or business.

A pastor, who was also a mortician, shared a story about one of his parishioners. He suggested to this woman to purchase life insurance for her young son. She did not see the relevance for it because he was so young, but eventually purchased a policy. A few months later, after the purchase, her sixteen year old son was in a car accident that claimed his life. This was an unfortunate situation but could have been much worse. The bright side to this story is that the mother was able to bury her son without a struggle, after his untimely death, because she'd listened to wisdom and purchased the policy.

Yes, you may spend your money on whatever you want, it's your choice, yet, often the wrong one is made as it relates to life insurance. What you do not know will later become rather expensive for you.

If you are a surviving spouse, you should ensure that your beneficiaries are changed on your life insurance policies from your spouse to someone else as soon as you receive a copy of the death certificate. By leaving a deceased person on your policy as a beneficiary can cause unnecessary delays in claims processing and the alternative of finding who would be entitled to the money, especially if a secondary beneficiary is not listed. Let's take a look at the various types of insurance.

This is only a basic review of insurance to assist you with selecting the best type for you and/or your family. It is highly recommended that you take some time to visit with a licensed insurance agent to acquire more detailed information.

So, how much life insurance do you really need? There are multiple factors to take into consideration when calculating the amount to purchase. There should be enough insurance to cover your salary times ten, or more based on your yearly debt, family size, children(s) college expenses, etc, in order to ensure an adequate lifestyle for whomever you would leave behind.

There are two types of term insurance: (a) decreasing term that drops the total face amount over time and (b) level term that the face amount remains the same throughout the life of the policy. This type of insurance may increase in payments every few years but caps off at a specific period of time, and then expires. The payments are usually lower than whole life insurance. You can have term life insurance for a five, ten, fifteen or twenty-year terms. These are the plans that I have personally reviewed but there could be other term periods.

My father had a number of life insurance policies and I would review them from time to time to ensure continued activity; he had several whole life and term policies that he maintained for many years. After his eighty-sixth birthday, I discovered that three of his policies had expired and were no longer in force. It was not a surprise because I knew that they were level term policies with the expiration date to occur after a specific age. But because he had a number of other policies, this discovery had little impact on the final amount. Many people do not expect to outlive any of their policies, but he did, by two years. Term policies are not bad to purchase but please ensure that you read the terms and understand the type of policy that you are purchasing and know what age the term will expire.

Universal life insurance has low payments like term life insurance but has cash value (investment) like whole life that will allow you to borrow from the face value, while you are still living. If you die before you pay back any amount that you borrowed, that amount will be subtracted from your policy amount. Universal life is a permanent policy with flexible premiums.

Fully underwritten life insurance policies requires a medical exam. With this type of life insurance product the examiner typically comes to your home and checks your height and weight and takes a small blood and urine sample. Why do life insurance companies test your blood and urine? Your lab results are then processed and the life insurance carrier offers you a policy based on your results, among other factors. In some cases, a physician's statement may be collected if the carrier feels more information is needed.

For healthy individuals the typical time it takes for the life insurance carrier to make an offer can be as fast as 48 hours. However, the normal time for a healthy individual is 2-4 weeks. For someone not as healthy it can take 4-6 weeks or longer. The one advantage with a fully underwritten policy is that for those who are healthy the savings can be substantial.

Whole life insurance has higher and more consistent premiums than the other types of insurances and will also accumulate a cash value. It does not expire after a period of time but stays in force for the life of the policy as long as the premiums never lapse and are made regularly. If the amount is over $50,000, a medical exam of the insured may be required in order to obtain insurance.

Variable life insurance is also a form of permanent life insurance coverage. These types of life insurance policies offer a death benefit, as well as a cash component.

However, with variable life insurance, the policyholder can take part in a variety of different investment options such as equities. This means that their funds have the opportunity to grow a great deal more than the funds in a whole life policy can. It also means that there can be more risk as funds are exposed to the ups and downs of the equities market.

It is important to note that while the policyholder can increase their funds based on market movements, their cash is not invested directly in the market. Rather, it is invested in "sub-accounts" by the insurance company.

With a variable life insurance policy, the death benefit may go up or down – however; it will not go below the set guaranteed amount. This is usually the original amount of death benefit that is purchased at the time of policy application.

No Medical exam policies do not require a life insurance health exam. Often, the difference in cost between a medical exam policy and a non medical exam policy are small. A no medical exam policy helps a client avoid some of the most common reasons for policies coming back at a higher rate class than applied: high cholesterol and high blood pressure. If you are concerned about your blood work then paying a few additional dollars might very well save you money once your lab results come back.

There was a husband who would not allow his wife to take out any insurance policy on him because he did not want her to marry another man with his life insurance money. She was told that she could take out a policy on him without his consent if it was below $50,000; she did not pursue it. Needless to say, he died before his wife, at a fairly young age and left her and their children destitute. This should not happen when finances are available to purchase a policy.

Guaranteed issue is a quick and easy type of life insurance. It is guaranteed issue life insurance so everyone within the required age bracket can qualify for this coverage. Typically, the amount you can qualify for will be from $5,000-$$30,000 depending on the carrier. Most come with a graded death benefit limitation which provides that the full death benefit will only be paid for natural causes after the policy has been in force for two or more years.

But, a note of warning is embedded in this form of insurance policy that states that if the primary insured dies before the 2 year graded death benefit limitation has ended, the policy will not pay out for natural causes. Most guaranteed issue policies will pay out the full amount in the first 2 years for an accidental death. And most have a 5-10% return on top of premium paid if the primary insured dies in the first two years of natural causes.

Accidental Insurance is another type of insurance all together. One of the worse stories that I have heard concerning Accidental Insurance was about a man back in the 1940's. As difficult as times were then, he managed to buy a few policies on his meager income as a gravedigger. He told his wife that if he died before she did, she would not have to worry about having any money because he had taken care of everything. When he died of a heart attack at the young age of forty-eight, to her dismay, she discovered that all of the insurance policies that her husband purchased were for accidental death. Her husband could not read and purchased the insurance because it was cheap. Needless to say, she had to make many adjustments for the next several years in order to raise their six children.

Accidental Insurance is sold sometimes individually and often in addition to other insurance as a rider for only a few dollars more. That means if someone dies from an accident, the beneficiary will not only receive the face amount of the insurance, but they will also receive the additional amount for death by an accident. So, if the regular policy was $300,000 with an accidental rider of $200,000, the beneficiary will receive a total of $500,000. If the person died of natural causes, the $300,000 will be the only amount disbursed. The $200,000 will be forfeited.

There are multiple companies that offer a varied amount of life insurance. AARP tends to focus on people who turn fifty years old and above; Globe Life has $50,000 in term insurance with your response to multiple health questions; Direct Term Life at AAA Life Insurance Company offers a term up to age 80 but has six-figure payouts; United of Omaha offers a whole life policy with smaller payouts of, $3,000, $5,000, $7,000 and $10,000 with no physical exams or health questions, with no increasing rates; there are also insurance coverage for newborns up to twenty-five years of age. Some of the premiums are as low as $2.17 per month based on the age of the child.

Typically, insurance companies will not payout the full face amount if the insured commits suicide within the first two years of the policy but will pay the beneficiary the premiums made by the insured. If the suicide is at two years and one day, there is usually a payout. As I said before, please thoroughly read your policy before you sign.

In the past, there were only a few types of life insurance policies from which to choose. However, as time has passed, many insurers have added to their array of product options. This has allowed individuals and families to find coverage that is best for them and their budgets. Ultimately you need to decide which type of life insurance policy is best for your needs. Understanding how each one works will make sure you make the right decision. With all of the many types of life insurance and carriers to choose from today, it can help to have an ally on your side who can help you choose the coverage that will fit your needs the best.

There was a woman who had faithfully paid for insurance for many years for herself but suddenly became very sick. The man that she was dating came in to so call, "care for her", and she trusted him with everything. He came for a few days with the appearance of assistance but then disappeared. When she passed, her family gathered all of her final paperwork and insurance policies to figure out what would be done. When the son of the woman called the insurance company, to his dismay, the policy had lapsed. It was discovered that the woman's boyfriend who came in under the pretense of assistance, took all of her money and did not pay any of her bills, which included the life insurance policy. Even though she paid her insurance faithfully, she did not have anyone that had the integrity to maintain her responsibilities during her incapacity. Quite naturally, the insurance company was not able to deliver a payout, which caused a major setback for the woman's family.

If you do not have adequate insurance, if your insurance has lapsed, or you do not have any insurance at all because you've misread the policy and thought that accidental coverage was whole life, your anger should not be taken out on the funeral home staff. For it is the responsibility of the deceased or a guardian of such, to ensure that sufficient coverage is acquired prior to this inevitable time in life, as no one lives forever. Moreover, there are multiple affordable plans that can fit any budget. Why not start today?

Chapter 4
Sample of Final Arrangement Documents

This section gives you an array of forms that will help you organize your funeral plans to not only ensure that your desires are known after you are gone but also that your loved ones will not be burdened with the task of guessing what you would have wanted during this time of grief. A Last Will and Testament overrides any verbal promises made by the decedent. It has been said, *"An oral promise is just as good as the paper on which it is written."* Basically saying, if it is not in writing, it is not valid.

When it is time to plan, do not put your funeral arrangements in your Will because the document will not be read until after the funeral services are over. Even though your arrangements should be listed separately, they are still important and should all be kept together.

Often, I look for opportunities to assist people where I can. The unfortunate thing that I have discovered is that many people do not want to be helped but rather live in confusion and disarray simply because they do not want to be told what to do.

In one situation where a Will would have been helpful is this: there was a couple who lived together for over thirty years as boyfriend and girlfriend but the husband was still married to someone else. He was separated all those years from his wife but never divorced her. When he died, the wife stepped in and took everything that belonged to her husband; money, property and his belongings. There was not a Will in place to leave anything for the girlfriend of over thirty years nor was she able to claim any of his things because she was not his wife; then, she died.

In another situation an organization for seniors was offering the opportunity to have a Last Will and Testament done for free, if the client was over the age of sixty. I shared this information with a few people who could benefit from the information and were also over sixty years old. One of them started the process but stopped, one of them said that they were going to let their children decide what to do with their final arrangements, which would be a mess, and the other person talked sarcastically to me about it as though they were going to live forever. To this day, regrettably, neither has completed this process and each of them is single. Please do not let this be you!

It is to this end that I have given three examples of Last Will and Testaments of: a single woman with children; a married person with children; and a single person with a deceased child. Each sample has various arrangements of information based on the assets that one has. From these samples, you will be able to tailor make your Last Will and Testament for your own personal property and assets.

I am not licensed to give legal advice, so it is highly recommended that you acquire a lawyer to assist you with this area of your life. Because of legal costs, many people utilize less expensive ways, such as online documents to draft your own, but you will need a notary public to validate your signature. Let's walk through the first sample.

Sample Will of a Single Woman with Children[3]

The first paragraph has the name and address identification of the person who the Will is for, the deceased. It also declares that it is the latest and final desires of the decedent and supercedes any other written documents that anyone else may have in their possession. (If someone else has another Will or a scrap of paper signed by you, the document with the latest date will be

---

[3] Scriven Law Offices, 1 Columbus Center, Suite 60, Virginia Beach, VA 23462. www.scrivenlawoffices.com

considered the final declaration). The second paragraph discloses the marital status and whether or not the decedent had any children, surviving or deceased. Each child is named for identification.

-Part I of this sample Will explains how the Executor/Executrix should ensure that all debts, taxes, funeral expenses are paid on the behalf of the decedent. An Executrix is a female and an Executor is a male who will be responsible for the final estate arrangements.

-Part II of this sample Will explains the distribution of personal property, furnishings, and various items to whomever the decedent named. These distributions should be implemented by the Executor/Executrix based on the request.

-Part III of this sample Will explains the disbursement of the residence and any other real estate property that the decedent owned.

-Part IV of this sample Will explains if there is any other real property or residue, in the interest of the decedent, it is also be left to a recipient.

-Part V of this sample Will explains the distribution of additional finances after all debts are paid. This could be from bank account savings, life insurance policies, etc. Each person is identified with a specific amount of distribution.

-Part VI of this sample Will explains somewhat of a description of what the Executor/Executrix is supposed to do with the decedents' property.

-Part VII of this sample Will explains restrictions to those who are stated as beneficiaries in this Will which does not allow assignments or pledges of their interest in the income from this trust.

-Part VIII of this sample Will reveals who the Executor and trustee will be along with the alternate representative in the event the primary choice does not survive the decedent or makes the decision to decline the requested responsibility. It waives an appraisal of the estate, bond for the Executor, trustee and the alternate representative. It further imparts all the authority to the Executor and the alternate representative that is granted by law.

The last few paragraphs are signed by the Testatrix (the person who is generating the Will), two to three witnesses (who are not included in the Will), and then the Notary Public (required).

Sample Last Will And Testament[4]
of
Jane Johnson Doe

I, Jane Johnson Doe, residing and domiciled in Disguise, Virginia 23555 do hereby make, publish, and declare this writing to be my Last Will and Testament. I hereby revoke all other wills, codicils, and other testamentary dispositions made by me before this date, without any limitations.

I am single. At the date of my execution of this Will, I have three living children, namely, Jean Doe Smith, Judy Doe Jones and John Doe, who are all competent adults as of the date of this Last Will & Testament.

PART I

I direct my Executor/Executrix, hereinafter named, to pay all my just debts and funeral expenses, including a suitable marker for my grave, without seeking exoneration or contribution from any beneficiary named in this Will, even though a beneficiary may be obligated with me in respect of any such debts. These payments should occur as soon as practicable after my death.

---

[4] Law Offices of Philip J. Forbes, IV, PC, 11171 Jefferson Avenue, Newport News, VA 23606. www.mfrblaw.com

All taxes assessed by reason of my death, whether or not the assets in respect of which such taxes have been imposed passed under this Will, shall be paid and charged as a cost of the administration of the estate passing hereunder.

My Executor/Executrix shall not require that any part of taxes due and payable from my estate be apportioned among the recipients of my estate property.

PART II

I give and bequeath my 2015 Jaguar to my daughter, Jean Doe Smith, if she survives me. If my daughter, Jean, does not survive me, then my Jaguar should be sold at top dollar and given to my children who survive me, share and share alike, with the rights of survivorship as at common law. All of the furniture, furnishings, household goods, silverware, china, and ornaments located in my residence at 123 Main Street in Disguise, Virginia are the property of my daughter, Judy Doe Jones, and I hereby acknowledge and confirm her ownership of all such items. All of my clothing, jewelry, personal effects, and all other tangible personal property owned by me at the time of my death, I give and bequeath to my children who survive me, share and share alike, with the rights of survivorship as at common law. I give and bequeath all monies in bank accounts or otherwise receivable for my benefit, except for the bequests that I make below, to my son John Doe, if he survives me. If my son does not survive me, then I give and bequeath all of my personal property consisting of all monies in bank accounts, or otherwise receivable for my benefit, to my other children who survive me and John, who are named above in equal shares, with the rights of survivorship as at common law.

PART III

I own my residence at 123 Main Street, Disguise, Virginia, and I give and devise in fee simple and absolutely to my children, Jean Doe Smith, Judy Doe Jones and John Doe, jointly, all of my interest in my residence and home owned by me at the time of my death.

All other real estate that I may own at the time of my death, regardless as to whether such real property is located in Virginia or any other place in the United States, I give and devise to all of my children who survive me, share and share alike, absolutely and in fee simple, in equal shares, with the rights of survivorship as at common law.

PART IV

The residue of my property, real and personal, wherever situated and however held, I devise and bequeath to my children, in equal shares, share and share alike, with the rights of survivorship as at common law.

PART V

I give and bequeath the following bequests in the amounts indicated thereof, after the payment of all debts and expenses associated with my estate, including my funeral expenses:

1. The sum of Twenty Thousand Dollars ($20,000) to my daughter, Jean Doe Smith, if she survives me. If my daughter does not survive me, then I bequeath this amount to both of my other children who survive me, share and share alike, with the rights of survivorship as at common law;

2. The sum of Twenty Thousand Dollars ($20,000) to my daughter, Judy Doe Jones, if she survives me. If my daughter does not survive me, then I bequeath this amount to both of my other children who survive me, share and share alike, with the rights of survivorship as at common law;

PART VI

Whenever, pursuant to the provisions of this Will, my Executor/Executrix is required to distribute all or any part of my estate to a person during his or her period of minority or incapacity, my Executor/Executrix shall, nevertheless, retain the property which would otherwise be required to be distributed to such person, and as trustee, and as a separate trust, may accumulate the net income therefrom.

My Executor/Executrix may distribute such property in any one or more of the following ways:

(a) by expending such property directly for the education, maintenance, or welfare of such beneficiary;

(b) by giving said property to the guardian of the person or of the property of such beneficiary; or

(c) by giving said property to a relative of such beneficiary upon the agreement of such relative to expend said property solely for the benefit of the beneficiary.

PART VII

To the extent that it is permitted by law, none of the beneficiaries of any trust created by this Will shall have the right to assign, pledge, or in any manner alienate his or her interest in either the income arising from or the principal of the trust. Also, no trust interests created herein shall be subject to any liabilities, execution, attachment, sequestration, or other legal process concerning any beneficiaries.

PART VIII

I name my son, John Doe, to be the Executor of my Will. In the event that my son shall decline to act or dies before I die, or for any other cause shall cease or fail to act, then I name my daughter, Jean Doe Smith, as the substitute Executrix. I name my son, John Doe Smith, as trustee of any trust created by this Will. In the event that my son, John Doe, shall cease or fail to act and serve as trustee, then I name my daughter, Jean Doe Smith, to serve as substitute trustee of any trust created by this Will.

I request that an appraisal of my estate be waived. Also, I request that bond and security shall not be required of my Executor or substitute Executrix or for the services of the trustee of any trust created by this Will. My Executor and trustee, and their successors, shall also have all of the powers contained in Section 64.1-57 of the Code of Virginia, as amended, which powers are hereby incorporated by referenced herein.

IN WITNESS WHEREOF, I have set my hand and seal to this Will and have initialed each page of this instrument in the margin next to the last line thereof and acknowledge the same to be my Will in the presence of the witnesses signed below on this _____ day of June, 2000.

_____(SEAL)
Jane Johnson Doe

Signed, acknowledged, declared, and published by Jane Johnson Doe, as and for her Last Will and Testament in our presence, we hereunto sign our names as witnesses to her signature to the foregoing Will and also identify the pages by placing our initials on the margins thereof on this _____ day of June, 2000.

_____OF_____

_____

_____OF _____

_____

_____OF _____

_____

COMMONWEALTH OF VIRGINIA)
) TO-WIT
CITY OF VIRGINIA BEACH   )

Before me, the undersigned authority, on this day personally appeared Jane Johnson Doe, along with _____, _____, and _____, known to me to be the Testatrix and the witnesses, respectively, whose names are signed to the foregoing instrument, and all of these persons being by me first duly sworn, Jane Johnson Doe, the Testatrix, declared to me and to the witnesses in my presence that said instrument is her last Will and that she willingly signed and executed it in the presence of said witnesses as her free and voluntary act for the purposes therein expressed; that said witnesses stated before me that the foregoing Will was executed and acknowledged by the Testatrix as her Will in the presence of said witnesses, who, in her presence and at her request, and in the presence of each other, did subscribe their names thereto as attesting witnesses on this day of the date of said Will, and that the Testatrix at the time of the execution of said Will, was over the age of 18 years and of sound and disposing mind and memory.

_____

Jane Johnson Doe (TESTATRIX)

_____

WITNESS

_____

WITNESS

_____

WITNESS

Subscribed, sworn, and acknowledged before me by Jane Johnson Doe, the Testatrix, and subscribed and sworn to before me by _____, _____, and _____, witnesses, this _____ day of June, 2000.

_____

NOTARY PUBLIC FOR VIRGINIA

My Commission Expires:

_____

My Registration No. is:

_____

Sample Will of a Married Person with Children

The first paragraph fill in the name and address identification of the person who the Will is for, the deceased. It also declares that it is the latest and final desires of the decedent and supercedes any other written documents that anyone else may have in their possession. It further establishes their maturity and state of mind at the execution of the Will.

-Article I discloses the marital status and whether or not the decedent had any children, surviving or deceased. The names of the spouse and children are named for identification.

-Article II directs the Executor/Executrix of the Will to ensure that all funeral expenses, taxes, interest and penalties are paid to resolve any debt on the behalf of the decedent.

-Article III directs that the disbursement of the residence and any other real estate property that the decedent owned would be initially devised (left) to the spouse but if the spouse does not survive the decedent the property would be distributed equally (share and share alike) between the surviving children as listed.

-Article IV directs the distribution of personal property, furnishings, and various items to whomever the decedent has named. This could possibly be mentioned on an Addendum with specific names and items but in the event a list is not present or delivered within a thirty (30) day period of time, it is assumed that none exists. Therefore the tangible property is distributed to the spouse of the decedent or the surviving children if the spouse is also deceased. These distributions should be implemented by the Executor/Executrix based on the requested desire. If there is any other real property or residue, in the interest of the decedent, it should also follow the same order. If any of the children are not survivors, then their child/children (lineal descendants) should receive the distribution in their place. However, if no child/children (lineal descendants) are survivors, the remaining tangible property would be equally shared between the decedents' surviving children.

-Article V directs a guardian appointment without bond for any minor children in the event that the spouse does not survive the decedent. It directs the spouse to become the Executor/Executrix or an alternative representative to serve without bond, in the event that the spouse does not survive the decedent.

-Article VI directs that if the decedent and the spouse dies within thirty (30) days of each other, it would be assumed that the spouse survived the decedent for the purpose of this Will. The Executor/Executrix will handle distributions related to minors and/or disabled beneficiaries but not to usurp the wishes of a spouse if they survive within the thirty (30) day window.

-Article VII discusses the intent of omission of heirs, anyone who claims that they are heirs and the disinheritance of any former spouses. If anyone feels that they have a right to contest the Last Will and Testament in any court, then provisions are made that they will not receive any entitlements under this Will. If by chance they are successful in contesting in any court, then they will only be awarded One Dollar ($1.00). This solidifies that the Testator/Testatrix was intentional about what they have in writing. Just a side note: *how ridiculous can one be to try to overturn the wishes of someone who knew exactly what they meant when they generated their Last Will and Testament? It is an outrage and a selfish act of entitlement on the part of the contester to contradict what is in black and white.*

None of the entitlements in this Will is transferable even if the beneficiary volunteers to do so and should be free from any other claims. In the event that a beneficiary contests any part of the Will, they will receive nothing, as if they were already dead before the decedent.

The Testator signs, along with two witnesses and the Notary Public, who verifies the validity of the signers. The example addendum list the names of beneficiaries and the articles that were bequest to them, which is signed by the Testator and the Notary Public.

LAST WILL & TESTAMENT
YOUR NAME

I, _____, who resides in the City of _____, County of _____, State of _____, being of full age and sound mind and memory, do hereby make, publish and declare this instrument to be my Last Will and Testament, hereby revoking all prior Wills and Codicils.

ARTICLE I.

The name of my spouse is _____, and hereinafter she shall be referred to in this Will as 'my spouse'.

I have living children as of the date of execution of this Last Will & Testament, namely _____, _____; and they, along with any they, along with any other child or children born to or adopted by me and my spouse after the execution of this Will, shall hereinafter be referred to in this Will as 'my children'.

ARTICLE II.

I direct that all of my debts, funeral expenses of administration be paid at my Executor's discretion from the income or principal of my estate as soon as practicable after the time of my death; all estate, inheritance, or other taxes imposed by reason of my death, together with interest and penalties thereon, shall be paid without apportionment from the income or principal of my residuary estate at my Executor's discretion.

ARTICLE III.
Real Property

Unless otherwise transferred or transferable by operation of law or by or through the terms of a written deed, I give and devise to my spouse, if she survives me, all of my interest in any and all real property and real estate maintained by me, whether as a residence (permanent or seasonal) or otherwise, together with all improvements thereon, but subject to any mortgages, liens or encumbrances. If my spouse does not survive me, I give and devise such real property to my children, in equal shares, share and share alike.

Tangible Personal Property

Written List. I may leave a written list signed by me disposing of certain items of tangible personal property. Any such list in existence at the time of my death shall be deemed incorporated herein by reference. This list will be designated as an "Addendum" to my Will. I shall attempt to attach this Addendum (in its most current version) to this Will. If no list is found and properly identified by my Executor within (30) days after my Executor is appointed, it shall be presumed that there is no such list or Addendum and any subsequently discovered list shall be ignored.

Distribution in Default of List. I give and bequeath all my tangible personal property not otherwise effectively disposed of (and/or not listed in my written Addendum) and owned by me at the time of my death to my spouse, if she survives me, otherwise to my children, in equal shares, share and share alike. My Executor may dispose of any tangible personal property, by sale or otherwise, which in the Executor's judgment or in the judgment of my children, should not be retained.

Residue

All the test, residue and remainder of my estate, be it real, personal, mixed, tangible or intangible property of whatever kind and whatever situated, not otherwise effectively disposed of (and not listed in my written Addendum), owned by me at the time of my death I give to my spouse, if she survives me, otherwise to my children, in equal shares, share and share alike.

Distribution to Children

In the event that any of my children predecease me or fail to survive me for a period of thirty (30) days, then the share of the estate that such deceased child would have received under this Will if living, I give, devise and bequeath to the lineal descendants of such deceased child. If any of my children predecease me and dies leaving no lawful lineal descendants living at the time of my death, then I give such deceased child's share to the survivors of my children.

ARTICLE IV.

If my spouse predeceases me and if it becomes necessary or desirable that a guardian of the Person and/or Estate for my children be appointed, then it is my wish and direction that any court having jurisdiction over such appointment appoint _____, as such guardian; and I request and direct that such person be permitted and authorized to qualify and act as such guardian in any jurisdiction even though such person may at the time be acting as the personal representative of my estate, without bond or security.

ARTICLE V.

I nominate my spouse, _____, as Executor of my estate. In the event that my spouse should predeceased me, or refuses or is unable for any reason to quality as Executor or complete the execution of this, my Last Will and Testament, then I nominate and appoint _____ as Executor of my estate.
I direct that no bond be required of my Executor or successor. To the extent permitted by law, the administration of my estate shall be independent of the supervision of any court. Any Executor of my estate shall have all of the powers from time to time conferred upon executors or administrators by law (except to the extent a power would conflict with this Will, in which ease the provision of this Will shall control), including the power to

assign, bargain, sell, convey, transfer, deliver, lease or otherwise dispose of and deal with any real, personal, tangible and/or intangible property belonging to my estate, upon such terms as my Executor shall deem best, without regard to the necessity of sale or other disposition for the purpose of paying debts, taxes or legacies; or to retain any or all such property not so required, without liability for any depreciation thereof; to make distribution or division of property in kind, or partly in cash and partly in kind, where necessary, in order to facilitate any distribution or division of assets under this Will, and to exercise reasonable discretion in determining the valuation of assets distributed in kind; to deliver to the parent, guardian or other person maintaining the minor beneficiary any property; to employ agents, accountants, brokers, attorneys at law, or other assistants determined by my Executor to be necessary for the proper settlement or administration of the estate or the sale of any part of the estate; to assign or transfer certificates of stock, bonds or others securities; to adjust, arbitrate, compromise, settle or abandon all claims in favor of or against my estate; to do any and all things necessary or proper to complete the administration of my estate, all as fully as I could do if living; and to execute, acknowledge and deliver any and all instruments of conveyance, transfer, powers of attorney, proxies or other paper writings by my Executor deemed necessary or incident to the plenary exercise of the powers and authority in this, my Last Will and Testament, vested in or conferred upon my Executor.

ARTICLE VI.

For the purposes of this Will, no person, except for my spouse, shall be deemed to have survived me if that person should die within thirty (30) days after my death. If my spouse and I die in such a manner that it cannot be determined in what order our deaths occurred, my spouse shall be deemed to have survived me.

If any individual beneficiary under this Will is a minor or is Disabled, distributions to such beneficiary may be made in whichever of the following ways as my Executor deems best:

(a) To the beneficiary directly;
(b) To the legally appointed guardian, conservator, or attorney-in-fact of the beneficiary; or
(c) To a custodian for a minor beneficiary under a Uniform Gifts to Minors Act or a Uniform Transfers to Minors Act.

A receipt for payment by any of the above persons will completely discharge my Executor in respect to that payment. This paragraph shall not be construed to permit my Executor to make any distribution to or for the benefit of my spouse in a form which would fail to qualify for the marital deduction.

A person is Disabled for purposes of this Will if either of the following is true:

(a) He or she has been adjudicated incompetent by an appropriate court; or
(b) He or she lacks the physical or mental capacity to manage his or her financial affairs, as determined by my Executor or by a physician familiar with the individual.

ARTICLE VII.

I have made this Will after giving thought and consideration to the same. I have intentionally omitted making provisions for any or all of my heirs who are not specifically mentioned and included herein. I specifically disinherit my former spouse(s), _____, from whom I am divorced. I specifically disinherit each, any or all persons whoever claims to be or who may lawfully be determined to be my heirs at law, except and unless such persons or entities are mentioned in this Will. If any such person unnamed in this Will shall contest in any court any of the provisions of this Will, then each , any and all such persons shall not be entitled to any devise, legacy, bequest or benefit under this Will. To any or all persons unnamed in this Will who are successful in contesting in any court any of the provisions of this Will, I hereby leave the sum of One Dollar ($1.00).

The interests of the beneficiaries under this Will shall not be transferable by voluntary assignment and, to the extent permitted by law, shall be free from execution, attachment, bankruptcy, levy and/or other procedures for the satisfaction of creditors' claims.

If any beneficiary named in this Will contests, in whole or part, this Will or in any manner attempts to have this Will declared invalid, such person shall receive no benefits or interests from this Will and my Will shall thereafter be carried out as if such person had predeceased me.

If any beneficiary or recipient of any bequest named in my Will disclaims all or part of a gift, that part or portion of the disclaimed bequest shall be distributed as if the disclaiming beneficiary or recipient had predeceased me.

Wherever the context so requires, the masculine, feminine or neuter gender shall include the other two genders, the singular shall include the plural and the plural shall include the singular.

If any of the provisions of this Will are deemed unenforceable, the provisions not deemed unenforceable shall remain in full force and effect.

(ADDENDUM AND ACKNOWLEDGEMENT ON FOLLOWING PAGES)

IN WITNESS WHEREOF,

I have hereunto set my hand to this, my Last Will and Testament, at _____,
(State)_____, on _____, 20_____.

Signature of Testator:

_____
(Your Name)

Signature of First Witness:

_____Dated: _____

Print name of First Witness here:

_____

Residence Address of First Witness:

_____

_____

Signature of Second Witness:

_____Dated: _____

Print name of Second Witness here:

_____

Residence Address of Second Witness:

_____

_____

Subscribed, sworn, and acknowledged before me by John Doe, the Testator, and subscribed and sworn to before me by _____, _____, and _____, witnesses, this _____ day of _____, 20_____.

_____

NOTARY PUBLIC FOR VIRGINIA

My Commission Expires:

_____

My Registration No. is:

_____

ADDENDUM
GIFTS OF PERSONAL PROPERTY

I hereby make gifts of the following items of personal property to those named below:

(Name of the recipient) – (Item giving away)
Example:

Aunt Cybil Jones	2012 Ford Explorer
Cousin Bee Shell	High School Class Ring
Nephew Bob Lo	$5, 550

Signature of Testator:

_____
(Your Name)

Subscribed, sworn, and acknowledged before me by John Doe, the Testator, and subscribed and sworn to before me by _____, _____, and _____, witnesses, this _____ day of _____, 20_____.

_____
NOTARY PUBLIC FOR VIRGINIA

My Commission Expires:

_____

My Registration No. is:

_____

Sample Will of a Single Person with a Deceased Child

The first paragraph fill in the name and address identification of the person who the Will is for, the deceased. It also declares that it is the latest and final desires of the decedent and supercedes any other written documents that anyone else may have in their possession. It further establishes their maturity and state of mind at the execution of the Will.

-Section A deals with the payment of debts and expenses for the decedent, including funeral expenses and current bills incurred by the estate.

-Section B the marital status and whether or not the decedent had any children, surviving or deceased. In this case the Testator is single and has a deceased child, whose name should be listed for identification.

-Section C the decedent opts to leave the personal property to their sister as there isn't any spouse nor any surviving children. If this was your current status, it is up to you to whom you would desire to leave your personal property. It could be a sibling, an aunt or uncle, parents, nieces, nephews, cousins, friends, pets, non-profit organizations or church members. It is completely up to you.

-Section D continues the distribution of residue, (remaining property).

-Section E establishes the intentional omission of naming of heirs to this estate. In this case, there aren't any heirs to omit.

-Section F speaks to the unnecessary contesting of the Will and the omission of any beneficiary or outside entity that refuses to accept this instrument as the final desires of the decedent. If any of the areas of contest becomes a matter, the Executor/Executrix is empowered to defend the Last Will and Testament of the decedent as the final and intended words.

-Section G lists the alternate beneficiary if no other beneficiary survives the decedent.

-Section I discusses the survivorship process if a beneficiary dies within thirty (30) days of the decedent.

-Section H explains the possibility of a simultaneous death provision. This is where the Testator and the spouse dies fairly close to the same time.

Section J lists who the Executor/Executrix and alternate Executor/Executrix will be. Whomever is selected as Executor/Executrix or an alternate, will be able to act with the same power and authority as the Testator of the Will, without bond.

The Testator signs, along with two witnesses and the Notary Public, who verifies the validity of the signers. The example gifts list the names of beneficiaries and the articles that were bequeathed to them, which is signed by the Testator and the Notary Public.

LAST WILL AND TESTAMENT
Of
Your Name

I, _____, of _____, _____, being of sound mind and memory, do make, publish and declare this my Last Will and Testament, hereby revoking all former wills and codicils made by me.

A. **DEBTS AND EXPENSES:**

I will and direct my executor to pay all legally enforceable debts, including the expenses of my last illness and funeral expenses, current bills and any and all other expenses incurred in administering my estate.

B. **FAMILY IDENTIFICATION:**

I am single.
I have one deceased child: _____

C. **PERSONAL PROPERTY:**

My personal effects, including automobiles, boats, sporting equipment, jewelry, furniture, furnishings, china, glassware, silver and household equipment (except those items which are specifically given to a beneficiary elsewhere in this Last Will and Testament in which case said specific gift shall take precedence over this paragraph) shall be distributed to my sister, _____. If my sister, _____, does not survive me, then I direct that my executor(s) divide my personal effects, as described above (except those items which are case said specific gift shall take precedence over this paragraph), among the following named beneficiaries or their issue by representation as the named beneficiaries or their issue by representation agree or, failing such agreement, in such manner as my executor(s) may deem equitable. If my spouse does not survive me and if my named beneficiaries or their issue by representation do not agree, I give my executor(s) full discretion to determine the division and distribution of the articles above referred to between my named beneficiaries or their issue by representation, and such determination shall be binding on all persons. The named beneficiaries for purposes of this paragraph are _____. If any beneficiary of mine is a minor at the time of such division, distribution shall be made to the person having custody of him or her for purposes of this distribution shall be made to the person having custody of him or her for purposes of this provision, and the receipt for such person of the distributable share of such minor shall fully and completely release my executor from responsibility for such personal property.

D. **DISTRIBUTION OF RESIDUE:**

I give, devise and bequeath all of the rest, residue and remainder of my estate and property, of whatever kind and wherever situated, owned by me at the time of my death, to my sister, _____. If my sister, _____, does not survive me, I give, devise and bequeath all of the rest, residue and remainder of my estate and property, of whatever kind and wherever situated, owned by me at the time of my death distributed to _____, if _____ survives me.

E. **HEIRS INTENTIONALLY NOT NAMED:**

There are no heirs.

F. **NO CONTEST PHRASE:**

If any beneficiary of this will or any trust created

under this will, singly or in conjunction with any other person:

1. Contests or otherwise objects in any court to the validity of any of the following documents or amendments thereto (hereafter "Document" or "Documents") or of any of their provisions:

   a. This Last Will and Testament,

   b. Any trust created pursuant to this Last Will and Testament,

   c. Any beneficiary designation of an annuity, retirement plan, IRA, Keogh, pension or profit-sharing plan or insurance policy signed by me,

   d. A buy-sell agreement signed by me,

   e. A family partnership agreement, limited liability company, or related operating agreement signed or established by me; or

2. Seeks to obtain an adjudication in any court proceeding that a Document is void, or otherwise seeks to void, nullify or set aside a Document (or any of its provisions);

3. Files suit on a creditor's claim filed in a probate

of my estate against the estate, or any other Document, after rejection or lack of action by the respective fiduciary;

4. Files a petition or other pleading to change the character (community, separate, joint tenancy, partnership, domestic partnership) of property already characterized by a Document;

5. Claims ownership of any asset held by me in joint tenancy, other than as a surviving joint tenant;

6. Files a petition to probate homestead in a probate proceeding of my estate;

7. Files a petition for family allowance in a probate of my estate; or

8. Participates in any of the above actions in a manner adverse to the estate, such as conspiring with or assisting any person who takes any of the above actions, then the right of such beneficiary to take any interest given to him or her under this will or any trust created pursuant to this will shall be determined as it would have been determined had such beneficiary predeceased the testator without surviving issue.

The executor is hereby authorized to defend, at the expense of the estate, any contest or other violation of this paragraph. Notwithstanding the foregoing, a "contest" shall include any action described above in an arbitration proceeding and shall *not* include any action described above solely in a mediation not preceded by the filing of a contest with the court. Notwithstanding the foregoing, this paragraph shall not apply so as to cause a forfeiture of any distribution otherwise qualifying for the federal estate tax marital deduction or charitable deduction.

G. **IF NO BENEFICIARIES SURVIVE:**

If no beneficiaries or alternate beneficiaries named herein survive, then I give the rest, residue and remainder of my estate and property, of whatever kind and wherever situated, owned by me at the time of my death to _____.

H. **SURVIVORSHIP PHRASE:**

If any beneficiary dies prior to the entry of an order, decree or judgment in my estate distributing the property in question, or within thirty (30) days after the date of my death, whichever is earlier, any interests which would have passed to said beneficiary under the provisions of this Last Will and Testament if such beneficiary had predeceased me, except that, if a 'Simultaneous Death Provision' is included in this Last Will and Testament or in any codicil thereto, the Simultaneous Death Provision shall take precedence over the provisions of this paragraph in regard to survivorship of my spouse. It is my intention that any property or interest which is distributed from my estate as a result of any transfer authorized by my executor prior to the death of said beneficiary will not be revoked or otherwise affected by the subsequent death of the distributor.

I. **SIMULTANEOUS DEATH PROVISION:**

If my spouse and I should die under such circumstances as would render it doubtful as to which of us died first, then it shall be conclusively presumed for the purposes of this Last Will and Testament that we died simultaneously.

J. **EXECUTOR(S):**

1. I constitute and appoint _____ executor of this my Last Will and Testament. I authorize and empower my executor to sell, transfer and convey and all of the property of my estate, real and personal, and to execute, acknowledge and deliver good and sufficient transfer and conveyances thereof.

2. If _____ is unable or unwilling to serve as executor, I constitute and appoint _____ as executor to serve with all rights and responsibilities given to the original executor(s).

3. If _____ is unable or unwilling to serve as executor, I constitute and appoint _____ as executor to serve with all rights and responsibilities given to the original executor(s).

4. In the administration of my estate, or of the property held in trust hereunder, my executor, as the case may be, shall have, in addition to the powers granted by law and by this Will, all of the powers set forth in Section 64.1-57 of the Code of Virginia, 1950, as amended, in effect on the date of my death: provided, however in order to avoid or eliminate unnecessary probate tax, my executor and any trustee hereunder, in its discretion, shall have the authority to waive the power to sell my real property. My executor(s) shall act without bond.

5. If no executor named in this will is willing and able to act, an executor or co-executors may be selected by the majority of adult beneficiaries named herein. The executor(s) so selected and appointed shall have all rights

and responsibilities hereinbefore given to the named executor(s).

6. No bond will be required of the executor.

IN WITNESS WHEREOF, I have hereunto set my hand and seal this _____ day of _____, 20_____.

_____
(Your Name)

The Testator signed, sealed and declared this as his/her will in our presence on the date shown above. At the Testator's request we have both signed our names as witnesses. All of this occurred at the same time and we and Testator were present together throughout.

_____
Witness   Address

_____
Witness   Address

COMMONWEALTH OF VIRGINIA)
) SS:
CITY OF NEWPORT NEWS)

Before me, the undersigned authority, on this day personally appeared _____,

_____, known to me to be the Testator and the witnesses, respectively, whose names are signed to the attached or foregoing instrument and, all of these persons being by me first duly sworn, _____, the Testator declared to me and to the witnesses in my presence that said instrument is his/her last will and testament, and that he/she had willingly signed or directed another to sign the same for him/her, and had executed it in the presence of said witnesses as his free and voluntary act for the purposes therein expressed; that said witnesses stated before me that the foregoing will was executed and acknowledged by the Testator as his/her last will and testament in the presence of said witnesses who, in his/her presence and at his/her request, and in the presence of each other, did subscribe their names thereto as attesting witnesses on the day of the date of said will, and that the Testator, at the time of the execution of said will, was over the age of eighteen years and of sound and disposing mind and memory.

_____
(Your Name)

_____
(Witness)

_____
(Witness)

Subscribed, sworn to and acknowledge before me by _____, the Testator, and subscribed and sworn to before me by _____ and _____, witnesses, this _____ day of _____, 20_____.

_____
Notary Public
My Commission Expires:

The gifts listed on this SPECIFIC Gifts form shall only apply if my beneficiary does not survive me.

SPECIFIC GIFTS UPON DEATH

Pursuant to the provisions of my Last Will and Testament which incorporates this specific gifts form by reference, I instruct the Executor/Executrix(s) to distribute the following gifts:

Description of Gift: _____
Desired Recipient and Relationship: _____
Dated: _____ Signed: _____

Description of Gift: _____
Desired Recipient and Relationship: _____
Dated: _____ Signed: _____

Description of Gift: _____
Desired Recipient and Relationship: _____
Dated: _____ Signed: _____

Description of Gift: _____
Desired Recipient and Relationship: _____
Dated: _____ Signed: _____

Description of Gift: _____
Desired Recipient and Relationship: _____
Dated: _____ Signed: _____

Description of Gift: _____
Desired Recipient and Relationship: _____
Dated: _____ Signed: _____

Description of Gift: _____
Desired Recipient and Relationship: _____
Dated: _____ Signed: _____

Sample Durable Power of Attorney

Some years ago, I was having a conversation about health and wellness, with an older gentleman (let's call him Joseph), that my husband and I knew, so we thought, rather well. He was single with no children.

As our conversation progressed, I asked Joseph was he prepared with his final arrangements and he responded that the bank has all of his arrangements. Taking a moment to process his response, I asked the same question again, which resulted in the same response. Then, I asked him who would speak for him if by some chance he was comatose or in a vegetable state. He responded that the bank will speak for him. At that time, I attempted to help Joseph understand that even though the bank may hold his final financial arrangements, he would also need to be prepared with a Durable Power of Attorney, Living Will, and an Advance Medical Directive with his desires for someone to convey his wishes. It would not be up to the person to make a decision but rather, they would relay his written desires to extend his life expectancy and handle his business because he couldn't.

Needless to say, the atmosphere suddenly turned hostile. Joseph raised his voice at me to ensure that I knew that the bank would speak for him. At that moment, I took a deep breath and retreated to my corner out of respect for my elder, knowing that he was not fully prepared for what was to come. About thirty (30) days later, we were notified that Joseph was rushed to the hospital and was in a coma. He was on life support and there were many tubes running in and out of his body. Unfortunately, there was NO ONE available to either speak for Joseph or handle the necessary business to assist with extending his life. Because he did not have a Durable Power of Attorney, Living Will, or an Advanced Medical Directive in place, assigning a responsible party to speak on his behalf, the hospital was able to acquire the necessary legal paperwork to pull him off of life support. In less than a day, Joseph was gone.

His finances were completely in order; shockingly, he left behind a million dollar estate and the appointed Executor to his estate was someone with whom he was not even on speaking terms because Joseph's selected Executor (who was much older than him), died a month after he died. How unsettling? Unfortunately, the bank has yet to speak for him. Let's take a look at the Durable Power of Attorney.

There is a Power of Attorney and a Durable Power of Attorney. According to an article by 360 degrees of Financial Literacy – American Institute of CPAs, the difference between the two forms are as follows:

> A Power of Attorney is a legal document that authorizes someone to act for you. You name someone known as an agent or attorney-in-fact (though the person need not be an attorney) who steps into your shoes, legally speaking. You can authorize your agent to do such things as sign checks and tax returns, enter into contracts, buy or sell real estate, deposit or withdraw funds, run a business, or anything else you do for yourself.
>
> A Power of Attorney can be broad or limited. Since the Power of Attorney document is tailored for its specific purpose, your agent cannot act outside the scope designated in the document. For example, you may own a home in another state that you want to sell. Instead of traveling to that state to complete all the necessary paperwork, you can authorize someone already in that state to do this for you. When the transactions to sell the home are complete, the agency relationship ends, and the agent no longer holds any power.

A regular Power of Attorney ends when its purpose is fulfilled or at your incapacity or death.[5]

A Durable Power of Attorney serves the same function as a Power of Attorney. However, as its name implies, the agency relationship remains effective even if you become incapacitated. This makes effective even if you become incapacitated. This makes the Durable Power of Attorney an important estate planning tool. If incapacity should strike you, your agent can maintain your financial affairs until you are again able to do so, without any need for court involvement. That way, your family's needs continue to be provided for, and the risk of financial loss is reduced. A Durable Power of Attorney ends at your death.[6]

For the purpose of this book, we will discuss the Durable Power of Attorney.

This following document is rather self-explanatory. As previously noted, it is designed for someone to act on the behalf of someone else especially if incapacitation or severe aging is a factor. Incapacitation could be considered comatose, immobile, home bound, a rehabilitation center or nursing home without the ability to drive. Severe again

---

[5] http://www.360financialliteracy.org/Topics/In-Crisis/Planning-for-incapacity/What-is-the-difference-between-a-power-of-attorney-and-a-durable-power-of-attorney

[6] Ibid.

could mean dementia, schizophrenia, Alzheimer's, or other conditions that affect the mental or reasoning capacities of an individual.

When this power is given to another, please ensure that the person selected is trustworthy and would act in your stead with integrity. They should administer decisions that are in your best interest and should keep your business from becoming delinquent at all costs.

There was a situation where two brothers argued over who would maintain a Power of Attorney for their ill father. The father was living with the oldest brother in Texas but grew tired and no longer wanted to care for him. Therefore the younger brother flew his dad to Tennessee in order to stay with him but the oldest brother did not want to release his power over their fathers' business. This became rather tedious for the younger brother in his care for their father. He had to contact his brother in Texas each time he needed to do something for their father: doctor's appointments, medicine, banking, etc. One day, the younger brother decided that he had had enough of the back and forth. He consulted an attorney, acquired a Durable Power of Attorney to manage the business of their father and the eldest son was ready to kill his brother over the change. The reason for the unnecessary irritation was that the younger brother discovered that the eldest brother was spending their fathers' money on his own personal things with little regard for the needs of their father, which did not end well. When the father passed, the eldest brother did not come to the funeral because he was angry with his brother, but called to know what the father had left him. When the Will was read, the father only left the eldest son $1.00 with the caption, *"Add this $1.00 to the amount that you have already stolen from me throughout the years and you will have your inheritance."*

Having a Power of Attorney is a huge responsibility as it is actually taking care of two households, depending upon the regular obligations that may be required of the person. When this document is signed, it should be signed in front of a notary public.

DURABLE POWER OF ATTORNEY

I, _____, appoint _____, my true and lawful attorney-in-fact, (hereinafter referred to as 'agent') for me and in my name, to do any and all acts which I could do if personally present. Until I am certified as incapacitated as provided hereunder, this Power of Attorney shall have no force or effect. All authority granted in this Power of Attorney becomes effective, it shall not be affected by any subsequent incapacity which I may hereafter suffer or the passage of time. For purposes of establishing incapacity, whenever two licensed, practicing medical doctors who are not related to me or to any beneficiary or heir at law by blood or marriage certify in writing that I am unable to manage my financial affairs because of mental or physical infirmity and the certificates are personally served upon me, then the agent named herein shall assume all powers granted in this Power of Attorney. However, even after receipt of the doctors' certificates, I retain the right to revoke this Power of Attorney at any time. Anyone dealing with the agent may rely upon written medical certificates or a photocopy of them presented to them along with the original Power of Attorney document, and shall incur no liability for any dealings with any designated agent in good faith reliance on said certificates and the original Power of Attorney document. This provision is inserted in this document to encourage third parties to deal with my agent without the need for court proceedings.

If _____ is unable or unwilling to act as agent, I designate _____ as agent to serve with all rights and responsibilities given to the original agent.

If _____ is unable or unwilling to act as agent, I designate _____ as agent to serve with all rights and responsibilities given to the original agent.

My agent(s) shall act without bond.

My agent may perform for me and in my name and on my behalf any act in the management, supervision, and care of my estate and affairs that I personally have authority to perform. My agent may exercise for me and in my name and on my behalf the powers enumerated below, which are intended to illustrate, and not to limit, the scope of this power. This power of attorney shall apply to all property owned by me, whether title is held as sole owner, as a joint tenant, as a tenant in common, as grantor or trustee of a revocable living trust, or otherwise.

A. SECURITIES: My agent may buy, sell, pledge, exchange, assign, option, or otherwise transfer any securities of any kind; deal with any broker, banker, or other agent; receive all dividends and interest payments now or hereafter due or payable to me from any security or other indebtedness or investment; vote stock and otherwise represent me at all meetings of shareholders or companies or corporations in which I have an interest; sign proxies or other instruments; tender my resignation as director or officer; subscribe to shares of stock, and execute request for payment of United States Savings Bond, and surrender paid securities and receive the proceeds thereof.

B. ACCOUNTS: My agent may open, continue, maintain, change, or close any account, including without limitation any checking or savings account, certificate of deposit, share account, and other like arrangement with any bank, trust company, savings bank, building and loan association, savings and loan association, credit union, or other financial institution; make deposits and withdrawals by check, draft, or otherwise; and endorse checks, notes, and drafts for deposit, collection, or otherwise.

C. <u>BENEFITS</u>: My agent may apply for and receive any government, insurance and retirement benefits to which I may be entitled. My agent may also exercise any right to elect benefits or payment options or to receive cash value in return for the surrender of any or all rights under any of the following: Life insurance policies, or benefits; annuity policies, plans or benefits; mutual fund or other dividend investment plans; and retirement, profit sharing and employee plans and benefits.

D. <u>DEEDS</u>: My agent may sign, execute, deliver and acknowledge such deeds, deeds of trust, covenants, indentures, agreements, mortgages, pledge agreements, notes, receipts, checks, bills of exchange, evidence of debts, releases and satisfactions of mortgage debts, judgment debts and other debts.

E. <u>OTHER PROPERTY, INCLUDING REAL ESTATE</u>: My agent may sell, exchange, option, and convey my real and personal property, wherever located; execute and deliver deeds of general warranty, with the customary covenants for such property; manage and control my real and personal property, wherever located; negotiate, execute, and deliver any leases of my property; demand and collect rents; buy every kind of property, real or personal; arrange for appropriate disposition, use, insurance, and safekeeping of all my property; settle, compromise, and adjust insurance claims; borrow money in my name, and to receive such loans by real estate mortgage or by other collateral. My agent may also purchase medical insurance for any dependent of mine.

F. TRANSFER OF ASSETS: My agent may transfer from time to time some or all of my assets to the trustee or trustees of any revocable trust that I may have established or may establish in the future, regardless of the extent or limitations on my beneficial interests in that trust, to be administered in accordance with the terms thereof.

G. OPERATION OF BUSINESS: My agent may continue the operation of any business belonging to me or in which I have a substantial interest for such time and in such manner as my agent may deem advisable or to sell or liquidate any business or interest herein, at such time and on such terms as my agent may deem advisable and in my best interests.

H. COLLECTION AND LITIGATION: My agent may demand and collect all property, real or personal, now or hereafter due, payable, or belonging to me; contest, compromise, settle, or abandon claims in my favor or against me; give receipts, releases and discharges; commence, pursue, or oppose any action, suit, or legal proceeding relating to any matter in which I am or may hereafter be interested; and compromise, settle or submit to judgment any such action or proceeding.

I. <u>TAXES</u>: My agent may represent me before any office of the Internal Revenue Service or the Treasury Department of the United States and before the tax department of any state, county, or municipality with regard to any and all tax matters with which I am concerned. In particular without limitation, my agent may represent me in connection with any federal income tax return, Form 1040, for all tax years between 1950 and 2050, inclusive; any federal gift tax returns, Form 709, for all tax years between 1950 and 2050, inclusive; any Virginia income tax return, for all tax years between 1950 and 2050, inclusive; and any Virginia gift tax return, for all tax years between 1950 and 2050, inclusive. My agent may perform all acts that I can perform with respect to any and all tax matters without limitation. My agent may prepare, sign, and file any tax return; prepare, sign, and file any power of attorney required by federal or state tax authorities, in particular without limitation Form 2848; receive originals of all notices and other written communications; negotiate and make compromises; file claims; receive, endorse, and collect checks; receive and examine confidential information; and take appeals, file protests, and execute waivers and closing agreements. My agent may consent on my behalf to have any gift made by my spouse considered as made by each of us under section 2513 of the Internal Revenue Code.

J. SAFE DEPOSIT BOX: My agent shall have access to any safe deposit box of mine (whether the box is held in my name alone, in my revocable trust, or jointly with another or others) wherever located, and may remove the contents and surrender the box on my behalf. Any institution in which a safe deposit box of mine is located is not liable to me or my heirs or estate for permitting my agent to exercise this power.

K. POST OFFICE: My agent shall be able to request and authorize the post office to forward my mail to whatever address my agent may deem advisable.

L. SOCIAL SECURITY: My agent may represent and act for me before the Social Security Administration of the United States, and any similar agency of a state or local government; collect all Social Security benefits due me; and make such arrangements in connection with Social Security benefits including without limitation Medicaid and Medicare as will facilitate their application to my care and support.

M. <u>EMPLOYMENT OF AGENTS</u>: My agent may employ and dismiss agents, attorneys, investment advisors, accountants, housekeepers, and other persons, and terminate any agency that I may have created at any time.

N. <u>FIDUCIARY POSITIONS</u>: My agent may renounce any fiduciary positions to which I have been or may be appointed, including, but not limited to Executor/Executrix, trustee, guardian, conservator, attorney-in-fact and officer or director of a corporation; to resign such positions in which capacity I am presently serving, and to file an accounting with a court of competent jurisdiction, or settle on a receipt or release or other informal method as my agent deems advisable.

O. <u>NOMINATION OF GUARDIAN</u>: In accordance with Virginia Statutes, as amended from time to time, I nominate my agent to serve as my guardian, conservator, or in any similar capacity to serve without bond or security.

P. ACCESS TO MEDICAL AND OTHER RECORDS:
My agent shall have the authority to obtain all of my medical records or other records, and shall have the authority to sign any authorization required by the Final Privacy Regulations issued pursuant to the Health Insurance Portability and Accountability Act (HIPAA) in order to obtain access to Protected Health Information about me, and any other consent or release that might be required to authorize the release, use or disclosure of confidential health information.

Q. SEVERABILITY: The invalidity of a provision of this power of attorney shall not affect another provision.

R. GIFTING: **This Durable Power of Attorney shall in no way be construed to grant the power to make gifts of my property to third parties or to the agent(s) as individual(s), nor to revise, revoke, or execute estate planning documents for me. This Durable Power of Attorney shall not be construed as granting a general power of appointment.**

S. COMPENSATION: My agent shall be reimbursed for all reasonable costs and expenses actually incurred and paid under this power of attorney. My agent shall act without compensation.

THIS POWER OF ATTORNEY SHALL NOT BE AFFECTED BY MY SUBSEQUENT DISABILTY, INCAPACITY, OR INCOMPETENCY.

I hereby declare that any act or thing lawfully done hereunder by my said agent(s) shall be binding upon me, my heirs, legal representatives, Executor/Executrix, and assigns.

IN WITNESS WHEREOF, I have hereunto set my hand and seal this _____ day of _____, 20___ in the City of _____, State of _____.

WITNESSES:

_____

_____

_____
(Your Name)

COMMONWEALTH OF VIRGINIA)

) SS:

CITY OF NEWPORT NEWS)

Personally came before me this _____ day of _____, 20____, the above named _____, to me known to be the person who executed the foregoing instrument and acknowledged the same.

_____

Notary Public

My Commission Expires:

Sample Living Will

Many have heard of the necessity of a Last Will and Testament but few know that a Living Will is also a necessity.

> This written document sets out how you should be cared for in an emergency or if you are otherwise incapacitated. Your living will sets forth your wishes on topics such as resuscitation, desired quality of life and end of life treatments including treatments you *don't* want to receive. This document is primarily between you and your doctor, and it advises them how to approach your treatment. Try to be as specific as possible in this document, realizing that you can't account for every possibility, which is where the durable power of attorney for health care comes in.[7]

To address the subject of resuscitation, you will notate whether or not you wish to be resuscitated. If you do not desire to receive this treatment, you would list DNR, which means Do Not Resuscitate on your medical records. From personal experience, a DNR is not as cruel as one would imagine. If you are a senior and your body is in a fragile state, chest compressions could leave permanent

---

[7] Enea, Scanian & Sirignano, LLP, White Plains, NY, http://www.estate.findlaw.com

damage and could assist in your demise. These methods should be carefully considered as to how you would expect your family to respond.

LIVING WILL

1. I, _____, being of sound mind, willfully and voluntarily state my desire that my dying may not be artificially prolonged if I have an incurable injury or illness. It is my desire to execute this document in order to permit my physician, family, and designated attorney(s)-in-fact to make decisions about the withholding or withdrawing of life support in accordance with my instructions which are provided herein under Paragraph 2.

2. Death is as much a reality as birth, growth, maturity, and old age. It is one certainty of life. If the time comes when I can no longer take part in decisions for my own future, let this statement stand as an expression of my wishes while I am still of sound mind.

If the situation should arise in which there is no reasonable expectation of my recovery from physical or mental disability, I request that I be allowed to die and not be kept alive by artificial means or heroic measures. I do not fear death itself as I fear the indignity of deterioration, dependence, and hopeless pain. I therefore ask that medication be mercifully administered to me to alleviate suffering, even though this may hasten the moment of my death. This request is made after careful consideration. I hope you, who care for me, will feel morally and legally bound to follow this mandate. I recognize this appears to place a heavy burden of responsibility upon you, but it is with the intention of relieving you of such responsibility and placing it upon myself, in accordance with my strong convictions, that this statement is made.

If I have checked "Yes" to the following, my attorney(s)-in-fact may have a feeding tube or other forms of non-oral nutrition and hydration withheld or withdrawn from me, unless my physician has advised that, in his or her professional judgment, this will cause me pain or will reduce my comfort. If I have checked "No" to the following, my attorney(s)-in-fact may not have a feeding tube or other forms of non-oral nutrition and hydration withheld or withdrawn from me.

Withhold or withdraw a feeding tube or other forms of non-oral nutrition and hydration

Yes ____   No ____

If I have not checked either "Yes" or "No", my attorney(s)-in-fact may not have a feeding tube or other forms of non-oral nutrition and hydration withdrawn from me.

3. I designate _____ my attorney-in-fact, under a durable power of attorney designation as permitted by Virginia Statutes, and hereby instruct my physician to consult with my attorney-in-fact to obtain consent for the withholding or withdrawal of life sustaining procedures or for the provision of care under the circumstances which exist at any time due to my medical condition. If _____ is unable or unwilling to act as attorney-in-fact then _____ shall act with all rights and responsibilities given to the original attorney-in-fact. If _____ is unable or unwilling to act as attorney-in-fact then _____ shall act with all rights and responsibilities given to the original attorney-in-fact.

In making this designation, I intend that this power of attorney shall not be affected by any subsequent disability or incapacity should that occur. If I have designated any other person to be my attorney(s)-in-fact over my estate, this designation is not intended to revoke that one.

4. If my care providers seek the assistance of a guardianship court with respect to life-sustaining procedures or other medical care decisions, I hereby state my desire that the attorney(s)-in-fact designated herein be appointed by the court as guardian(s) of my person, and be given authority to make such medical care decisions regarding my person as may be permitted under Virginia Statue.

5. I expressly waive any liability for any medical personnel which could in any way arise from their compliance with carrying out my wishes pursuant to this document.

6. I expressly state that this Living Will is in addition to my Last Will and Testament dated _____, or any codicils thereto.

Dated this_____ day of _____, 20____.

Signed: _____
       (Your Name)

I know declarant and I believe the declarant to be of sound mind. I am not related to the declarant by blood or marriage, and am not entitled to any portion of the declarant's estate under any Will or Trust of the declarant. I am neither the declarant's attending physician nor an employee of the attending physician or of the inpatient health care facility in which the declarant may be a patient and I have no claims against the declarant's estate at this time.

WITNESS: _____

WITNESS: _____

ADVANCED MEDICAL DIRECTIVE

I, _____, willfully and voluntarily make known my desire and do hereby declare:

If at any time my attending physician should determine that I have a terminal condition where the application of life-prolonging procedures would serve only to artificially prolong the dying process, I direct that such procedures be withheld or withdrawn, and that I be permitted to die naturally with only the administration of medication or the performance of any medical procedure deemed necessary to provide me with comfort care or to alleviate pain. (OPTION: I specifically direct that the following procedures or treatments be provided to me:

_____

_____

_____

In the absence of my ability to give directions regarding the use of such life-prolonging procedures, it is my intention that this advance directive shall be honored by my family and physician as the final expression of my legal right to refuse medical or surgical treatment and accept the consequences of such refusal.

OPTION: APPOINTMENT OF AGENT (CROSS THROUGH IF YOU DO NOT WANT TO APPOINT AN AGENT TO MAKE HEALTH CARE DECISIONS FOR YOU).

I hereby appoint _____, of
Address:_____
Telephone number: _____
as my agent to make health care decisions on my behalf as authorized in this document. If _____ is not reasonably available or is unable or unwilling to act as my agent, then I appoint _____, of
Address:_____
Telephone:_____
to serve in that capacity. If _____ is not reasonably available or is unable or unwilling to act as my agent, then I appoint _____, of
Address:_____
Telephone:_____
to serve in that capacity.

I hereby grant to my agent, named above, full power and authority to make health care decisions on my behalf as described below whenever I have been determined to be incapable of making an informed decision about providing, withholding or withdrawing medical treatment. The phrase "incapable of making an informed decision" means unable to understand the nature, extent and probable consequences of a proposed medical decision or unable to make a rational evaluation of the risks and benefits of a proposed medical decision as compared with the risks and benefits of alternatives to that decision, or unable to communicate such understanding in any way. My agent's authority hereunder is effective as long as I am incapable of making an informed decision.

The determination that I am incapable of making an informed decision shall be made by my attending physician and a second physician or license clinical psychologist after a personal examination of me and shall be certified in writing. Such certification shall be required before treatment is withheld or withdrawn, and before, or as soon as reasonably practicable after, treatment is provided, and every 180 days thereafter while the treatment continues.

In exercising the power to make health care decisions on my behalf, my agent shall follow my desires and preferences as stated in this document or as otherwise known to my agent. My agent shall be guided by my medical diagnosis and prognosis and any information provided by my physicians as to the intrusiveness, pain, risks, and side effects associated with treatment or non-treatment. My agent shall not authorize a course of treatment which he knows, or upon reasonable inquiry ought to know, is contrary to my religious beliefs or my basic values, whether expressed orally or in writing. If my agent cannot determine what treatment choice I would have made on my own behalf, then my agent shall make a choice for me based upon what he believes to be in my best interests.

OPTION: POWERS OF MY AGENT (CROSS THROUGH ANY LANGUAGE YOU DO NOT WANT AND ADD ANY LANGUAGE YOU DO WANT).

The powers of my agent shall include the following:

A. To consent to or refuse or withdraw consent to any type of medical care, treatment, surgical procedure, diagnostic procedure, medication and the use of mechanical or other procedures that affect any bodily function, including, but not limited to, artificial respiration, artificially administered nutrition and hydration, and cardiopulmonary resuscitation. This authorization specifically includes the power to consent to the administration of dosages of pain relieving medication in excess of standard dosages in an amount sufficient to relieve pain, even if such medication carries the risk of addiction or inadvertently hastens my death;

B. To request, receive, and review an information, verbal or written, regarding my physical or mental health, including but not limited to, medical and hospital records, and to consent to the disclosure of this information;

C. To employ and discharge my health care providers;

D. To authorize my admission to or discharge (including transfer to another facility) from any hospital, hospice, nursing home, adult home or other medical care facility for services other than those for treatment of mental illness requiring admission procedures provided in Article 1 (37.2-800 et seq.) of Chapter 8 of Title 37.2; and

E. To take any lawful actions that may be necessary to carry out these decisions, including the granting of releases of liability to medical providers.

Further, my agent shall not be liable for the costs of treatment pursuant to his authorization, based solely on that authorization.

OPTION: APPOINTMENT OF AN AGENT TO MAKE AN ANATOMICAL GIFT (CROSS THROUGH IF YOU DO NOT WANT TO APPOINT AN AGENT TO MAKE AN ANATOMICAL GIFT FOR YOU).

Upon my death, I direct that an anatomical gift of all or any part of my body may be made pursuant to Article 2 (32.1-289.2 et seq.) of Chapter 8 of title 32.1 and in accordance with my directions, if any. I hereby appoint _____ as my agent, of _____, to make any such anatomical gift following my death. I further direct that:

<u>Declarant does not want to make an anatomical gift or organ, tissue or eye donation (declarant's directions concerning anatomical gift or organ, tissue or eye donation).</u>

This advance directive shall not terminate in the event of my disability.

By signing below, I indicate that I am emotionally and mentally competent to make this advance directive and that I understand the purpose and effect of this document.

Date:_____Signature: _____

The declarant signed the foregoing advance directive in my presence.

Witness:_____

Witness:_____

Chapter 5
Sample Obituaries

After the death of a loved one there are many ways to memorialize their legacy. One of the ways is through the use of an obituary, itemizing their lifetime achievements. Traditionally, an obituary is placed in the local newspaper to notify others of your loss. If cost is an issue for this type of advertisement, a shorter snapshot of only the necessary information is printed, while the longer version is later printed on a bulletin or program for a memorial service.

Because we are in the age of technology, there are various inexpensive ways in which to share this type of news to alert the masses, ie., Facebook, Twitter, Instagram, Snapchat, etc., just to name a few. Word of mouth is still the best way to let others know what has taken place and what the future plans and location will be for any ceremonial memorials.

If a church is selected to be the location of the service, it is best to ensure you are familiar with the policies and rules of that particular institution. Churches are autonomous and typically carry their own rules about services for members and non-members. This should be the first thing to be done prior to selecting a church as a venue.

Cost could also be a factor for a location and may require fees to be paid up front.

It is understood that at this difficult time you may or may not be able to focus or gather your thoughts in order to organize information about your loved one but I will give you a tip on how to pre-manage this task.

Over the years, I have kept a folder on my computer of obituaries of myself, my husband, children and some of my loved ones that I know, if I survive them, I will have to assist in some way with the administration of their final arrangements.

Each time I attend a funeral of someone else or whenever something major happens in our lives, I update my own obituary, and the obituaries of my other loved ones. This keeps the information up-to-date in case someone else will have to pull data together for my life and legacy.

Although all memorial services do not require a printed program, these are a couple of sample obituaries that you can tailor to the life of a loved one. If the service is held in a church, oft times there are bereavement committees that will assist the family with setting up the obituary to ensure that a consistent flow is achieved.

Also, depending on your budget, the availability of printing, and the amount of information cf the decedent that you will use, you may choose to use the formats of either a trifold, bi-fold, booklet style, etc. After this section, we will address one of the simplest styles, the double-sided format.

The first obituary is more of a traditional obituary with church trimmings and all. It is set up in the form of a multiple page program.

The cover has the deceased name, birth and death date along with a photo, (either more recent or perhaps one that people would recognize the individual during their better days); the date and location of the funeral services and the name of the officiant.

On the inside left of the program, the service starts with the procession of the family, musical prelude, and any song or solo that is planned. Some songs have musicians, which may or may not know how to play the song that the singer will sing; some will sing "a cappella", which can be great as long as the soloist is not tone deaf and changes pitches repeatedly; and some may use a soundtrack. The drawback for a soundtrack is if there is a glitch in the soundtrack itself and it doesn't play appropriately when necessary, then there will need to be an alternative solution. In either case, pre-planning is essential.

In a church setting, the Old and New Testament readings are traditionally read by a minister or an official of the church but it is always the choice of the family who they decide will read the Scriptures and conveyed to the officiant. Whoever is selected to read the Scriptures, please ensure that they can read well in a public setting, not just because they are Uncle Tony's favorite nephew.

The acknowledgements reader should also be a well-read person. One of the funeral home staff may assist the family in this area. Sometimes there are many cards, letters and correspondence sent to the family, but to be courteous to the guest attending, all of them should not be read publically to avoid a long, drawn out service. The family can decide prior to the service to read one to three cards and letters. I have found if there are multiple letters, then reading one or two of them would be in order, then reading the names of the rest of the senders could be read for acknowledgement and to save time. The family can read each piece of correspondence among themselves, in their entirety, after the funeral is over.

The reflections section is the time people are given to remember the deceased, by funny stories and memories that are not offensive to the dead. In my past experiences with funerals, this area has often turned out to be a "funeral flunk". There were those who reflected on times that were meant to be private, but for some reason that information was shared with the public during reflections and shined a different light on the person to be memorialized. This is never acceptable. One should not give reflections just to brag or measure "how close" they were to the deceased in relation to other guest or family members by calling them "pet names" that were only reserved for a few or some undisclosed, irrefutable matter that should die with the individual; this is not a contest of closeness, as the deceased, perhaps in some way touched the lives of most or all of the people attending the services.

This day is about the deceased; they are the star of the show (so to speak). No one should usurp their will of a 20-minute reflection, especially if there is someone else giving the eulogy. Those who are giving reflections should honor a maximum time limit of 2-3 minutes out of respect for others who will come behind them. However, this type of behavior can be "nipped in the bud" if pre-selection of those who will give reflections is done. This will shut down some of the unexpected unpleasantries and can help prevent people who are not true friends of the deceased from spewing unscripted garbage over the remains. Some families will have a wake or a service before the final service to give people who want to memorialize and reflect on the deceased, the opportunity to do so in a more conducive setting.

If the deceased was a member of the church, a workable order for reflections would include: a selected family member, friend, church member and member of the clergy to speak on the behalf of each category.

The time limit for reflections is also a factor. If the deceased is to be buried, typically there is a specific timeframe in which the cemetery allots for burial. Therefore, a lengthy service can become an issue.

The obituary is usually silently read while soft music plays a chorus and a verse of something. If the service was running long in time, I have witnessed an officiant simply say, *"You have had plenty of time to read the obituary, let's move on."* He was actually right! The obituary was the first thing that most of the people read as soon as they received the program.

A eulogy is simply remembering a person the way they were and it does not take a preacher to eulogize a person but someone who perhaps was in a close relationship or a trusted individual who would not divulge personal secrets or disparaging situations. For the traditional church funeral, the minister uses this opportunity to point people to Christ by (a) highlighting the Christian life of the person in conjunction with a scriptural theme or episode (b) pointing persons to Christ in light of what being a believer did for the deceased and for those who were blessed by their life, especially if they were a faithful member of the church. The Christian eulogy should be more than just snippets of the pleasantries of the person's life offered by a family member or friend. Of course, if the person was not a Christian or had no spiritual adherence, then that is another situation entirely.

It is not unheard of to have another minister or a well-spoken friend to eulogize the deceased. It would be awesome if this too is pre-planned, if not, please seek assistance from those who were indeed closest to the deceased. In cases like this, I have witnessed family members choosing a eulogist that they wanted instead of who the deceased would have preferred because the family members had personal issues with the eulogist; this could prove to be problematic.

The video slideshow has been something added to memorial services in these latter years. It is a conglomeration of pictures of the deceased and their activities over the years. This works very nicely while soft music or a song that fits the life of the deceased is playing. All establishments are not equipped to accommodate this type of request but worth the trouble of asking in advance.

Although a final viewing of the remains can be done at the gravesite before the casket is let down, a viewing at the end of service is often requested by the family. However this can be an exhausting experience even after the services are over. This is sometimes considered the final viewing of the deceased and can easily end in a grieving session that can last a little longer than one may desire.

If you would like to have pictures, color or otherwise, you may add an insert to the middle of the program without changing the order of what you already have.

The remainder of the program including the obituary, the pall/floral bearers, thank you's, interment and professional entrusted services are self-explanatory.

You can replace the printed information from this book with the information of the deceased individual when an obituary is needed. If there is some information that does not apply to the individual, omit what is not needed and add what is. This is a basic guide to generate a program for your loved one in case you are not able to think about specifics during your period of grieving.

Another important nugget is, if someone outside of the funeral home was hired to render a special service, such as, a minister, musician(s), soloist(s), please ensure that someone is assigned to compensate them either before the service starts or by the end of the service. It is not fair to have them standing around waiting for their compensation because everyone is still crying.

A Celebration of Life
For
John Jack Doe, Sr.
Sunrise December 5, 1970   Sunset May 10, 2050

PICTURE GOES HERE

Thursday, May 17, 2050
11:00 o'clock am
St ABC Church
2000 Anywhere Blvd
Surprise, VA 12345

Bishop I. M. Apreacher, Pastor
Officiating

ORDER OF SERVICE

Musical Prelude

Processional……………………………………………....Family

Song of Comfort

   Old Testament - Psalm 133……(Someone who reads well)
   New Testament – John 14:1-6…(Someone who reads well)

Prayer of Consolation

Acknowledgments………………(Someone who reads well)

        Reflections by selected individuals below
                    (2 minutes please)

   Family……………………………………...XYZ Family
   Friend……………………………………….XYZ Friend
   Church Member………………..XYZ Church Member
   Clergy……………………………………….XYZ Clergy

Obituary…………………Soft Music…………(Read Silently)

Song

Eulogy………………………………………Bishop Apreacher
                St ABC Church, Surprise, VA

        Video Memory & Final Viewing

Recessional……………………………………………........Family

OBITUARY

On May 10, 2050, a husband, father, grandfather, brother, and friend, John Jack Doe, Sr. departed this life at Waters Hospital, Surprise, VA, after an extended illness.

John was born December 5, 1970 in Peachtown, VA to the late James and Jane Greir Doe. He attended Peachtown Public Schools and later attended Peachtown State University for a few years. He was affectionately known as "J. Jack" by those who knew him well.

His most memorable recognitions and achievements were: President of Peachtown Community Committee and also held the position of Secretary. He was also the President of Peachtown City Alumni. John accepted Christ in his life at an early age, and was a member at CBA Church.

John was the father of three children. He was married to Jean Grier Doe, on March 12th, 1995, in Apple, VA and to this union three children were born.

John is preceded in death by his father, James Doe, mother, Jane Grier Doe, one brother, Joe Doe.

He is survived by his devoted wife of 55 years, Jean Grier Doe, his sons, John Jack, Jr. (Lisa), and Jim Doe; his daughter, Jill Doe; one brother: Jackie; one sister: Joan (Lee); four grandchildren, and an abundance of special nieces, nephews, cousins and in-laws.

If I can help somebody as I pass along
If I can cheer somebody with a word or a song
If I can show a stranger that he's traveling wrong
Then my living shall not be in vain.

Written by Alma B. Androzzo

<u>Pall Bearers</u>
Male Family Members

<u>Floral Bearers</u>
Female Family Members

<u>Interment</u>
Grass Bay Cemetery
Surprise, VA

<u>Acknowledgments</u>
Jean and family acknowledges with sincere thanks and appreciation to Bishop Apreacher & St ABC Church and others for all acts of kindness that have been expressed during this difficult time.
May God richly bless each of you!

<u>Special Thanks To</u>:
The Medical Staff at Waters Hospital

<u>Professional Services Entrusted To</u>:
North West Funeral Home
Surprise, VA

***

A repast will be held for immediate family only at St ABC Church, Surprise, VA

Insert of Photos of J. Jack Doe

Memorial Service
For
Dr. Jill Jean Smith

Sunrise June 23, 2007   *Sunset February 19, 2037*

[PICTURE GOES HERE]

Saturday, February 25, 2037
6:00 pm
Christmas Eve Funeral Chapel
Proper, NC 54321

Memorial Service

Family Gather

Reflections

    (Family & Friends will eulogize Jill)

Poem by Janie Smith   (Jill's Niece)

There will not be a burial; Jill was cremated as requested. Repast will be held at the JKL Community Center on Main Street.

Jill's Life

What a vivacious person Jill was; she enjoyed a full life. Although she was just a young lady when she passed, she had zero regrets. She traveled to all fifty states and all of the continents, with Europe being her favorite stop. Jill ate everything in sight but managed to maintain a girlish figure of 125 lbs, consistently.

She worked at Fossil Investments and was very rich. Jill did not want to be married as she felt that marriage would refocus her goals and hold her hostage from her dreams as she was a free spirit.

Jill had a PhD in Financial Management and wanted you to know it.

She was a ward of the state and never knew her parents or any other family members. She would say, "all those who love me is my family."

She is survived by her dog, Justice, who is now very well off.

Sample Poems to Use

Momma

Momma – A cool breeze in dry weather

Momma – A light at the end of the tunnel

Momma – A conversation without words

Momma – A sweet thought in times of peril

Momma – A friend who I will miss dearly

Dr. I. Franklin Perkins

Dad

Who can walk a mile in your shoes

No one that I have found

I heard you carried me to the nursery

Somehow knowing that you would never let me down

You were always there for me

When times were really tough

You were my confidant, protector and friend

When things were really rough

So now I say, "Goodbye my friend"

Although my heart is sad

It gives me great pleasure to say

That you were my Dad

Dr. I. Franklin Perkins

Thank You For Sharing

Although you are gone away
Your memory I will keep in my heart
The life that you lived made such impact for so many
I will always cherish the moments we had together
They mean so much to me
Thank you for unselfishly sharing yourself
Dr. I. Franklin Perkins

You Will Be Missed

The moment I heard the news, I was crushed inside
I could not imagine what I would do
No one could replace your smile or your words of love
You really cared for others and gave your all
For this, I can only appreciate what I've learned
You will be missed
But I will still see you in the lives of those
that you've touched
Dr. I. Franklin Perkins

Life

L – Living a full life without regrets

I – Initiating lifelong friendships

F – Forgetting life's past hurts

E – Enjoying the quality of life

This will be my memory of you.

        Dr. I. Franklin Perkins

I Will See You Again

It's all in ones' perspective

How we deal with the loss of a friend

It's not really easy to endure the hurt

As my heart continuously tries to mend

So I asked, "Why did you leave me here

In a world that is full of hate"

I gather your response would be "Love while you can"

Those feelings I cannot abate

Therefore, I write out my sorrows and all of my pain

With a felt tipped blue pen

Knowing that our separation is only temporary

Because one day I will see you again!

        Dr. I. Franklin Perkins

Although I Cry

Although I cry,
Understand that they are tears of joy
I'm glad that you are no longer in pain
I'm glad that you are free from wordly pressures
I'm glad that you were in my life
Who could ask for much more than that?
Although I cry,
Understand that they are tears of relief
My fears are gone
My anguish has vanished
My strength will be renewed
I am resolved with the past, present and future,
Although I cry.
Dr. I. Franklin Perkins

The Garden of Feelings

As I walked through the garden, there were so many beautiful flowers, some reds, some blues, some greens and yellows; such an array of beauty.

However, some were withered which troubled me so.

When I looked closer I realized that each withered flower bore the feelings that I experienced at the loss of you.

I saw grief, loneliness, heartache, depression, and pain but I did not want those feelings anymore.

So, I picked the withered flowers and threw them away.

Then I began to nurture the strong colorful flowers in the garden. They bore happy memories, love, peace and your undying legacy. Those flowers are the only flowers that I will cultivate in the future.

Dr. I. Franklin Perkins

My Love

My love for you is undeniable

You hold the key to my heart

Every second we spent together

Was worth it

We created memories

Both great and small

We took memorable pictures with our eyes

As we held hands during our walks and sweet

conversations

I still feel your hand in mine

As I retain our most intimate moments.

Dr. I. Franklin Perkins

When Time Runs

When time runs out
I can no longer share with you
When time runs out
I can no longer have your ear
When time runs out
I can no longer feel your touch
When time runs out
It's too late for me to show you I care
Time has run out

Dr. I. Franklin Perkins

Bibliography

http://www.360financialliteracy.org/Topics/In-Crisis/Planning-for-incapacity/What-is-the-difference-between-a-power-of-attorney-and-a-

Enea, Scanian & Sirignano, LLP, White Plains, NY, http://www.estate.findlaw.com

Law Offices of Philip J. Forbes, IV, PC, 11171 Jefferson Avenue, Newport News, VA 23606. www.mfrblaw.com

Scriven Law Offices, 1 Columbus Center, Suite 60, Virginia Beach, VA 23462. www.scrivenlawoffices.com

Williams, T. B. *After the Storm Workbook/Journal (Recovering From Personal Loss and Grief)*, 1st Edition, Copyright 2012.

Order Information

To contact Dr. Perkins for
speaking engagements, visit the website at:

ItsmeDrIFP.org

You may also order paperback books,
donate and/or view itinerary
at the website above.

Please email: (itsmeDrIP@aol.com)
or call for bulk orders

Like our page on Facebook at: It's Me Dr IFP Ministries

Follow us on Twitter: @itsmeDrIFP

Mailing Address is:

Dr. I. Franklin Perkins
P.O. Box 9523
Hampton, VA 23670
757-825-0030

www.ingramcontent.com/pod-product-compliance
Lightning Source LLC
Chambersburg PA
CBHW050552300426
44112CB00013B/1880